We become the people we follow.

You might find that statement extreme. Most of us want to think of ourselves as original, so let me explain. I'm not a handy person, so the challenge of fixing things around the house is rather overwhelming. When the dishwasher breaks, the ice maker quits or the van is acting up, I can read a manual, but the illustrations never look quite like the real thing. I have called people and asked them to walk me through some troubleshooting steps, but with different makes and models it ends up with the blind leading the blind. Then YouTube came along and changed everything. I simply type in the problem along with the make and model and inevitably a video pops up with an "expert" making the repair step by step. I carefully watch that person go through the steps and when I think I can duplicate what they are doing, I am ready to attempt the repair myself. If things don't go well, I review the video, observe each step and imitate them exactly.

I am amazed at what YouTube has allowed me to accomplish simply through the art of imitation. I still follow a couple of those do-it-yourself types. I shouldn't be surprised though since we are natural-born imitators. Like most boys, I studied what my dad did and duplicated it. He put Brylcreem in his hair and combed it over, so I put Brylcreem in my hair and combed it over. When I was old enough to milk cows, I watched his every step and then followed suit. Through the years, I was his Mini Me. The very best parts of his life are duplicated in me.

Following people can also work against us. Imitating certain drivers has produced a number of bad habits for me. I accelerate too quickly and brake too hard. And yes, I am that driver who doesn't signal when they are going to change lanes. Certain family members I respect (who shall remain anonymous) have a diet soda addiction, and I have the same. The question is not: "Are you a follower?" We all are! The question is: "Are you following the best role model?" Following Jesus, who models true life, is the heartbeat of a disciple.

In the very beginning, God created human beings in his very image. He formed Adam and Eve with the ability to think, feel, act, create and purpose as he did. When he walked in the cool of the evening with them, they got to see firsthand who they were created to be and how they were to reflect that image. Unfortunately, sin changed all that. Instead of imitating the one in whose image we were made, we became followers of broken people and broken systems. Our thinking, feelings and actions no longer reflected the image of a glorious creator. The more we imitated the world's brokenness, the more broken humanity became. No matter how many laws, rules and regulations people were bound with, they had no one to follow who reflected who we were created to be.

That all changed the moment Jesus was incarnated into this world. Here for everyone to follow was the fullness of the image we were created in. In fact, Jesus himself said that in seeing him, we see the Father. Then he gave a most radical invitation of two simple but life-changing words: Follow me. Twenty times in the four gospels Jesus calls people to pick up a cross, sell their possessions, give up their livelihood, leave an old way of life, forget the dull and boring and follow him.

That call to come and follow was more than an invitation to casually hang out. It was more than a call to an extreme adventure. Those were the words used when a rabbi invited a new student to come, sit as his feet as a disciple and study life together.

Ray Vander Laan was one of the first of the popular writers to describe this specific invitation. The desire of every parent in Jesus' day was that their son would become a rabbi, but that was not easy. A boy would have to do well in school and then around the time he was 13 he would seek out a rabbi from whom to learn, one gifted in education, reputation and inspiration. After making his choice, the student would then wait for the teacher to choose him. If the student did not look promising, the rabbi would send him home to get married, have babies and pray that one of those babies would grow to be a rabbi. If the rabbi saw potential in that student, a simple invitation was given: Follow Me. From that moment on, the student became a disciple devoting himself not only to learning from the rabbi, but to imitating him.

The Mishnah, a Jewish collection of rabbinical writings gave this command to disciples: *Let thy house be a meeting-house for the wise; and powder thyself in the dust of their feet; and drink their words with thirstiness.* Rabbi Ben Yoezer urges disciples to keep their home open for teaching, to be thirsty for the words of a teacher and to cover themselves in their dust. What does that mean? Having given up everything, a disciple was to follow a rabbi so closely they would be coated in the dust that rabbi kicked up.

I smile when I think of that. Raised on a farm, I would

help my dad with some of the tasks. On certain occasions, he would drive the hay baler, and I would ride behind taking the bales and piling them on the wagon attached to that baler. By the end of the day, I was nearly unrecognizable covered in the gray dust and green chaff my dad's driving kicked up. From a distance, you could not tell us apart.

After following in the dust of a rabbi, a disciple would be unrecognizable. He was completely different than when he started. He now looked a lot like the rabbi. From the way they lived, you couldn't tell a student from a teacher. Because every part of the rabbi's life had something to offer, a disciple would follow as close as he could to hear what his teacher said and do what his teacher did. More than that, the disciple would want to feel as the rabbi felt, think as he did and live as he did. All that was for a twofold purpose. First the disciple would become a Mini Me of the rabbi. Second, he would likewise one day call a disciple to follow him and pass on what he had learned.

When Jesus called the twelve disciples, it is possible some of them had been rejected by other rabbis. Perhaps they had been told they were not smart enough or good enough to be a rabbi. But Jesus' two simple words changed their lives. Two words they may have longed to hear, but never had. Follow me.

Do you ever wonder why they jumped so quickly at the possibility? When everyone else had rejected them, Jesus believed in them. They left everything to get covered in his dust. They watched what Jesus did and imitated it. They watched him talk to people and imitated that. They watched him reach out to the poor, the lost and the disadvantaged and did so themselves. They watched him pray and asked him to teach them to pray. During those three and a half years, they came to imitate the head, heart, hands and feet of the Savior.

The stakes in this process were high. They knew one day, when the rabbi said they were ready, it would be their turn to go and make disciples. Between his resurrection and ascension, Jesus commissioned the disciples:

> *Jesus came and told his disciples, "I have been given all authority in heaven and on earth. Therefore, go and make disciples of all the nations, baptizing them in the name of the Father and the Son and the Holy Spirit. Teach these new disciples to obey all the commands I have given you. And be sure of this: I am with you always, even to the end of the age." (Matthew 28:18-20)*

Having followed Jesus for over three years, these men were completely covered in dust. They had the head, heart, hands and feet of the Savior and now sought to call others to follow them so they in turn could would become the head, heart, hands and feet of the Savior. They made disciples who made disciples, who made even more disciples.

The church talks a lot about discipleship. We throw that term around with very little clarity on what it means or what it looks like. We don't provide a very clear picture of what it means to be a disciple. How do you know if you are a disciple? How do you know if you are ready to disciple another person? Is there a way to know what a disciple looks like?

If a disciple is someone who gets right in there and follows as close to Jesus as they can, imitating everything he does, then they are someone with the head, heart, hands and feet of Jesus.

A disciple has the
- **head** of Jesus, thinking and acting like him
- **heart** of Jesus in that their emotions are patterned after Jesus
- **hands** of Jesus reaching people as Jesus reached, discipling others as he discipled
- **feet** of Jesus, able to take their stand, resting in the same power and resources that Jesus had

Right now, you may be trying to imitate someone. It could be your sister who is always a darling wherever she goes. It might be the soccer mom you envy or the business associate who seems to have it all. It might be the coach of your team or the salesperson of the month. The person you are following so closely might just be someone on social media. Let me ask you: What will the results be of following that person? More stress? Great disappointment? Failed expectations? Hurt feelings?

I invite you on a fresh journey through the scriptures to follow Jesus as the disciples followed him. As we examine the dust that got caked onto the disciples, my prayer is that you will come to have the head, heart, hands and feet of the Savior. Our journey following Jesus will teach us forty important ways a disciple follows the Savior to mirror the way he lived. For each of us there is an opportunity to get covered in some dust by applying those discipleship truths to real life.

But there is more to Jesus' prayer. "Teach these new disciples to obey all the commands I have given you." You really can't follow closely as a disciple and not be discipling someone else.

One caution. During the journey, Jesus told the twelve disciples. "Whoever wants to be my disciple must deny themselves and take up their cross and follow me." (Matthew 16:24b) And for many, their journey ended at a roughhewn X-shaped instrument of death.

If we are to follow him, we can't do it empty-handed. We have to pick up a cross and allow ourselves to be emptied through our willingness to shatter all the strongholds of our life, put to death all the brokenness that plagues us and lay siege to our feeble expectations. Only then can the dust of the author and giver of resurrection life, transform us through the power of the Holy Spirit.

COVERED IN DUST

I. HEAD - Having the Mind of Christ
1. Gospel-centered
2. Discipleship-oriented
3. Familiar with the Father
4. Aware of the Deceptiveness of Sin
5. Focused on the Savior
6. Empowered by the Cross
7. Fixed on the Future
8. Character-driven
9. Spiritually-disciplined
10. Family-oriented
11. Servant-hearted
12. Kingdom-minded

II. HEART - Feeling like Jesus
13. Loved by the Father
14. Loving of Others
15. New in Christ
16. Forgiven
17. Forgiver
18. Citizen of Heaven
19. Steward of God's Riches

III. FEET - Standing and Resting in Christ
20. Filled with the Spirit
21. Directed by the Spirit
22. Rooted in Christ
23. Discerning of Spiritual Realities
24. Victorious in Battles
25. Devoted in Prayer
26. Listener in Prayer
27. Intercessor in Prayer
28. Student of God's Word

29. Doer God's Word
30. Communicator of God's Word
31. Possessor of a Biblical Worldview

IV. HANDS - Reaching Like Jesus
32. Growing My Heart for the Lost
33. Sharing Christ with the Lost
34. Defending the Existence of God to the Lost
35. Defending the Authority of Scripture to Reach Others
36. Defending the Uniqueness of Jesus
37. Conversing about God and Suffering
38. Using My Spiritual Gifts to Reach Others
39. Using My Resources to Reach Others
40. Making Disciples who will Reach the World

CHAPTER 1

HEAD - Having the Mind of Christ

"You look like a man on a mission!" I hear that lot from people who want me to pause and engage with them in conversation, particularly in the church lobby between services. Now I love talking and often stop to meet new people or catch up with others at Calvary, but there are times that I am indeed on a mission. I have a time crunch and don't want to be delayed. During those moments I have to keep my eyes forward and my feet moving to get to a newcomer's class, solve a problem or retrieve something from my office.

Without a doubt, Jesus was a man on a mission. While it was a purposeful mission, it was also a balanced mission. He balanced tasks with people. He balanced urgency with patience. He balanced grace with truth. He balanced doing with being. He packed a lot of activity into a day and was still able to find rest. He lived far more intentionally than I ever could.

He lived purposely because He lived in truth. He embodied a life that reflects the truth of living the way God intended for us. Jesus taught his disciples to think. In fact, he challenged their conventional thinking in many ways, inviting them to see the world as God originally intended.

In order to be a follower, we have to have the mind of Christ. Thinking as Jesus thought is critical for a disciple, as it will inform every area of our life. As we will see, to adopt a Jesus-minded worldview, we will come to know and live out the truths about the nature of God, humanity, salvation, our character, our future and our mission. We have to learn them in our head so they can come forth in our life.

As you begin, would you pray that you might have the mind of Christ, open to thinking and living as he did?

Gospel-Centered

Scripture records Jesus' passion for sharing the gospel and inviting people to receive the good news of the Kingdom. As he started his ministry, Luke records his passion. "But he said, 'I must proclaim the good news of the kingdom of God to the other towns also, because that is why I was sent.'" (Luke 4:43) You can't help but sense the priority Jesus had to communicate the gospel and the urgency to get the word out.

What is the good news? The good news is that we in ourselves are not good enough to do anything to inherit eternal life. The Old Testament laws of rules and regulations were insufficient. During the Sermon on the Mount, Jesus said, "Do not think that I have come to abolish the Law or the Prophets; I have not come to abolish them but to fulfill them." (Matthew 5:17) In John 3, Jesus tells Nicodemus that he did not come to condemn the world, but to forgive the world. That culminated in his death on the cross as a once-for-all-sacrifice and his resurrection from the grave. He is the way, the truth and the life. There is no other way to the Father but through him. (John 14:6)

A disciple is first and foremost profoundly changed
14

by the gospel. They have stopped trying to prove themselves worthy before God and rest in the good news of God's grace and forgiveness. Living it out becomes a priority, and looking for opportunities to share the reason for a changed life becomes part of the fabric of a disciple's life. A disciple recognizes that on the cross Jesus accomplished everything we will ever need. We become people grateful for the cross.

Because he fulfilled the law, the disciples saw Jesus not only speak the gospel, but they also saw him live out the gospel. Following so closely to Jesus, they saw him take every opportunity to extend grace, mercy and forgiveness to those who opened their heart to him. They saw the change gospel-living made in the life of a Samaritan woman who found new purpose. They saw it in a woman who found new life after being caught in an adulterous relationship. They saw it in the sorrow on Jesus' face when people refused to accept the message.

I would expect that most people who have picked up this book have already made a decision to follow Jesus, but that may not be the case. Perhaps you are reading this and have not embraced the good news of Jesus and surrendered to him. This would be a great time to do so.

Religion speaks of the ways we can try to be good enough to be accepted by God. It is filled with activities that will assuage our soul and help us connect to a spiritual realm. You may be surprised that Jesus preached against religion. Instead, he invites us to a relationship. God knew that we could never do enough or be good enough to get to Heaven. So, Jesus did it for us. He paid the price for our sin, shame and guilt on the cross. He rose again three days later to prove he is the author and giver of life. He invites us into a relationship with him. He wants to walk with us, talk to us, inform us and shape us. In other words, he is calling us to be his disciples. It is an invitation to be with him and to become like him. Come to him now.

A Christian is one who rests and stands in what Christ has done. John writes, "Whoever has the Son has life; whoever does not have the Son of God does not have life." (I John 5:12) Do you have the Son? If you do, you have confidence that you have life in him.

Get Dusty

If you have never invited Jesus into your life, there is no better time than right now. To do that, you can pray like this:

"Dear Jesus, I have spent my life following different people, beliefs, values and practices in the hopes of finding fulfillment and happiness. But I know you are the only source of those things. You came and gave your life on the cross for me. There is nothing I can do to be accepted by God because you have done it all. Come into my life and be Lord of my life. Help me to walk in the grace of what you have done every day."

If you have already given your life to Christ, then right now thank him for the grace you have received. Make sure you tell someone what you have experienced. Memorize 1 John 5:12 (above) and whenever doubts about your faith surface, remember those words. You have life because you have the Son.

Discipleship-Oriented

While Jesus communicated the gospel to great crowds, He spent the majority of his time discipling a few. Much of the gospels speak of the investment Jesus made into the lives of these twelve men. In fact, the largest section of John's gospel records Jesus' personal conversations with his twelve disciples before He was crucified. Jesus was committed to making disciples. He called the twelve to follow him, and they did. He invited the rich young ruler to leave everything and follow him; his refusal caused Jesus great sorrow. Jesus even broke convention in having a woman, Mary, sit at his feet while she learned from him. Sitting at the feet of a teacher was a term used to describe one who was a disciple.

Jesus knew that investing in a few who would then invest in a few was a more effective strategy than speaking to thousands. His invitation to Peter and others was: "Come, follow me," Jesus said, "and I will send you out to fish for people." (Mark 1:17) More than calling the disciples to learn from him, he equipped them to make disciples as well. It was this commitment to discipleship that launched the church. After his ascension, it was not the crowds who launched a movement and changed a world. It was 120 people, led by 11, who had been most deeply impacted by Jesus. These were people who left everything to follow him and who would then go on make disciples of their own.

When I look at my life, more has been done through the people I have spent time with than all my public ministry. I think of the churches that have been pastored, the mission fields changed and the community ministry done for Jesus through the people I have walked with over the years. Just like compound interest maximizes profits, investing in a few pays great dividends.

A disciple by definition is someone who has chosen to imitate the head, heart, hands and feet of Christ in order to affect the life of another. They are already thinking of who they might impact.

Get Dusty

Let's stop for a moment. Before we get further in this discipleship material, what are your intentions? If you are reading this for your own interest, to see if there is anything in discipleship that you have missed or to try and scratch an intellectual itch, then may I humbly suggest that you put this book away and look for something else?

But if you are eager to duplicate the life of Jesus you are imitating, then please read on. Who will you ask to follow with you? Would you be praying now who that person might be? Maybe you already know them. Perhaps you have been spending time with them. If you are a parent, your children are your first priorities. Jesus called you to be a fisher of men so you could go out and impact people. Who will you ask?

Familiar with the Father

A. W. Tozer wrote: "What comes into our minds when we think about God is the most important thing about us." Jesus was continually challenging the disciples' limited view of God. Perhaps most surprising was the way he talked so intimately about God as his Father. He shared with the disciples about his Father's nature, his Father's abilities and his Father's character. The purpose of his life was to glorify the Father and the Father would be glorified in him. These twelve men already had a picture of God from their upbringing, but Jesus was going to share so much more with them. The more they understood about him, the more authentic their spiritual life was.

Jesus taught about the nature of God. God is Spirit. He is wholly "other," not like us at all, and we cannot put our own limitations on him. (John 4:24) He is God, and we then are not. Yet he is also eager to pursue a relationship with us. (John 3:16) He is light. In him there is no darkness. He has no hidden or ulterior motives. He is completely trustworthy.

As Spirit, God is not limited in what he can or cannot do. His knowledge is not limited. He knows everything, including things no one else knows like date and time when Christ will return. (Matthew 24:36) Space and time do not limit him. Because he is everywhere, nothing you say or do is hidden from him. There is nowhere you can go where he is not. Jesus said you can go into a room, shut the door and pray, and your Father will hear you. (Matthew 6:5-6) He is not limited in his power. There is nothing he cannot do. (John 16:23) The disciples could rest knowing God was always with them, would always teach them and would still their storms.

Through Jesus' teaching and actions, the disciples were taught to live differently, knowing the attributes of God.

They submitted joyfully to God because He is sovereign. (Matthew 19:26)
They sought to live holy because God is holy. (Luke 1:49)
They treated others fairly because God is just. (Luke 18:7)
They extended mercy because God is merciful. (Luke 15:22-24)
They trusted his word because God is faithful. (Luke 1:49)
They boldly approached him because He loves to give good gifts. (Matthew 7:11)
They knew he and his word would never lead them

astray because God is true. (John 17:17)

We won't pray with power if we don't know the one we are praying to. We won't trust his word if we don't understand the author. We won't worship passionately if we don't know the one who deserves our praise. We won't respond with gratitude if we are unsure of who blesses our lives.

Get Dusty

What you believe about God may be the most important thing about you. A disciple chooses every day to act with intention out of what is true. Do you know these and other truths about God? Are lingering doubts about his character, his ability or his love holding your actions hostage? A disciple takes that cross they are carrying and annihilates those wrong beliefs, to walk in the likeness of Christ. Take one attribute of God this week and make a decision about how you can order your life around that.

Aware of the Deceptiveness of Sin

Correct thinking about God is critical, but so is a correct understanding of ourselves. Until we know our true nature and our true brokenness because of sin, we will never fully appreciate the Father's love and the Son's sacrifice. As the disciples followed the interactions and teachings of Jesus, they came to a new understanding of just how broken and fallen we are. While Jesus came to reveal God, he also came to deal with our broken sinfulness. At his conception, the angel told Joseph to name him Jesus because he would save people from their sin. (Matthew 1:21) His followers knew people needed to be rescued.

Sin enslaves us. Jesus taught that sin puts us in bondage. "Jesus replied, 'Very truly I tell you, everyone who sins is a slave to sin.'" (John 8:34) Without the forgiveness and freedom of Christ, we are imprisoned by sin.

Sin also blinds us. While we think that we can trust our conscience, sin is so deceptive. The Father of Lies blinds us to the reality of who we are. The more we pursue a sinful life, the greater the deception will be. (John 12:39-40) This is why we need the scriptures and trusted people to help us see our true selves, beyond our sin's self-deception.

Sin prohibits the work of God in our life. In the parable of the sower, Jesus says God's word gets scattered on different soils in our heart. Like weeds that choke out good grain, sin chokes the fruit of truth in our life. (Luke 8:14)

In his teachings, Jesus was troubled by five recurring sins. *Do we want to number them?*

He warned against spiritual pride. Jesus told about a Pharisee and a tax collector standing in prayer together. The Pharisee who had a high place in society prayed a prayer of thanksgiving that He was not like the sinful tax collector. That spiritual pride kept the Pharisee's prayer from being heard. It was the tax collector, who humbly knew that he was a sinner, who had his prayer heard by God. (Luke 18:9-14)

He warned against hypocrisy. In particular, he railed against the hypocrisy of the Pharisees whose outer life presented an image of holiness yet their inner life was a mess. "Woe to you, teachers of the law and Pharisees, you hypocrites! You clean the outside of the cup and dish, but inside they are full of greed and self-indulgence." (Matthew 23:25) Jesus urged us to stop pretending. Only when we are honest about our sinfulness, can we truly deal with the root issues of our life.

Jesus warned against impurity. Whatever we fill our minds and hearts with will eventually come out in our life. He taught if your eye or your hand is going to cause you to sin, then you need to do something about it. Pluck it out or cut it off. Take drastic measures to protect yourself since sin will eventually blind and bind you. (Matthew 5:29)

Jesus warned against a lack of concern for people. Jesus had a habit of stopping and helping the people He saw in need. He told a story of how a Levite and a Rabbi had walked past a man who had been beaten and thrown into the ditch. They should have stopped to help. Surprisingly, it was a Samaritan who did stop to help. (Luke 10:25-37) Jesus was bothered by religious people who were more concerned with how they looked than caring for people. A disciple cannot let indifference take root in their heart. The gospel has to come out through a love for people.

Jesus warned against unbelief. Rarely did he criticize his disciples except for their lack of faith. It was their lack of faith that prohibited them from driving a demon out of a young boy. Jesus told them with the faith of a mustard seed they could accomplish much. (Matthew 17:17) This is why an understanding of the Father's character is so important. The more we know, the greater the faith.

Sin always has consequences and leads to separation from God. It does not separate us from God's love, though, which is why the passionate love of God compelled him to give his son for us. His mission was to come and to seek and save the lost. (Luke 19:10) A disciple understands sin is such a significant barrier to God that only the sacrifice of the blood of Jesus can deal with it. (Mt 26:28) God does not overlook sin, but gave his son to pay the price that we could not pay.

Get Dusty

"If we confess our sin, He is faithful and just to forgive us our sin and cleanse us from all unrighteousness." (I John 1:9) Ask the Holy Spirit to search your life. What sin does he bring to your mind? Be honest with God about that; be honest with yourself about how that keeps you in bondage. Make a conscious decision to change that behavior and then actually change it. Don't be afraid to ask for help or accountability to do that.

Focused on the Savior

Who is Jesus? A disciple has to be able to answer this fundamental question since most people won't follow someone they don't know. Discipleship is the ongoing journey to know Jesus more and more. Jesus wanted the disciples to be clear on who he was, so one day he asked them who they thought he was. Peter finally piped up and said that he was the Christ! He was the Son of God! It was upon that truth that the church was built. As the disciples followed, they heard him claim many things about himself.

Jesus claimed he had been with God from the beginning. John begins his gospel with these words: "In the beginning was the Word, [referring to Jesus] and the Word was with God and the Word was God." (John 1:1)

Jesus claimed that he was one with the Father. (John 10:10) This rattled the Jewish leaders who believed claiming to be God was blasphemy. Yet they were always troubled because the works that He did resembled the works of God. Because he and the Father are one, we can learn a lot about the Father by looking at Jesus. If we have seen Jesus, we have seen a glimpse of the Father. (John 14:9) Jesus showed the love, power, compassion, peace and authority of the Father. We see not only the Father's character in Jesus, but also the Father's glory. The glory of God's love was manifested on the cross. (John 17:1-5)

Jesus claimed that he was without sin in this world. He, who was a divine person, took on the flesh of humanity through the virgin birth. While he was tempted fully as we are, he was without sin. It is one thing to claim to be without sin; it is another to actually be without sin. But no one could find fault with him. "Can any of you prove me guilty of sin? If I am telling the truth, why don't you believe me? Whoever belongs to God hears what God says. The reason you do not hear is that you do not belong to God." (John 8:46-47)

Jesus claimed that he was able to forgive sins. But Jesus forgave not only sins done to him, but also the sinfulness of people. * When a sinful woman came to a party and anointed Jesus with tears of repentance, Jesus responded with forgiveness.

> Then Jesus said to her, "Your sins are forgiven." The other guests began to say among themselves, "Who is this who even forgives sins?" Jesus said to the woman, "Your faith has saved you; go in peace." (Luke 7:48-50)

He demonstrated his ability to forgive sin by performing other miracles. These outward healings pointed to the inner healing of forgiveness.

Jesus claimed to be the Messiah. Israel had been waiting for God's chosen and anointed person. They were looking for someone who would be the prophet speaking God's words to them, the priest who would lead them to a perfect relationship with God and the king who would rule mightily and peacefully over them. Jesus was that Messiah coming with a kingdom that was here now, but not fully until the end of the world. Most missed Jesus as the Messiah, but he claimed he was. (John 4:26)

Jesus claimed that he, as the Messiah, would die and rise three days later.

> *Jesus took the Twelve aside and told them, "We are going up to Jerusalem, and everything that is written by the prophets about the Son of Man will be fulfilled. He will be delivered over to the Gentiles. They will mock him, insult him and spit on him; they will flog him and kill him. On the third day, he will rise again." (Luke 18:31)*

Jesus claimed be a king; he spoke of a kingdom that was not of this world. At his trial, he told Pilate that he was king.

> *Then the whole assembly rose and led him off to Pilate. And they began to accuse him, saying, "We have found this man subverting our nation. He opposes payment of taxes to Caesar and claims to be Christ, a king." So, Pilate asked Jesus, "Are you the king of the Jews?" "Yes, it is as you say," Jesus replied.*
> *(Luke 23:1-3)*

Jesus claimed that he would return to judge the world and bring the world under his authority. He would establish a kingdom that would never end.

> *When the Son of Man comes in his glory, and all the angels with him, he will sit on his throne in heavenly glory. All the nations will be gathered before him, and he will separate the people one from another as a shepherd separates the sheep and the goats.*
> *(Matthew 25:31-32)*

He claimed to be the only way to God. Jesus stated that he was the way, the truth and the life, and no one would come to the Father but through him. (John 14:6) The exclusivity of this claim has troubled and offended people from the time it was spoken. In a world of tolerance, it seems unthinkable there could only be one way. This, however, is the defining statement of the Savior. When he said he was the only way, he was either lying or being truthful. He can't be partially telling the truth and worthy to be followed. No one comes to the Father God but through him.

Note - As disciples, we can forgive others for the sins they commit against us, but we cannot absolve someone of their sin. Only God can do that.

Get Dusty

A disciple devotes their life to knowing Jesus. There is no greater pursuit than pouring through the scriptures, reading the gospels and learning about the one they are following. Which claim of Jesus stood out to you today? What one life change would show you are taking that claim seriously in your life?

Empowered by the Cross

A wealthy and powerful businessman came to Jesus asking what he needed to do in order to have eternal life. We don't think a lot about eternal life these days as we are so busy trying to build heaven here on earth. But there comes a time, often near death, when people wrestle with this same question. Is there something next, and will I experience it? Have I done enough to get there? Is God pleased with me? Salvation is more than getting the next life; it is being rescued today from the power and bondage of this sinful world.

Salvation has always been a gift from God, given by grace through a person's faith. In the Old Testament, the people trusted that God would save them through their observance of the rules and the sacrifices of the Old Testament. Jesus came to change that. Salvation would still be by grace through faith but now it would be faith that the sacrifice of Jesus on the cross fulfilled the same requirements as those Old Testament sacrifices.

During Jesus' public ministry, he taught five simple truths about salvation.

Truth #1

God wants every person to be saved. Early in his ministry, one night a man named Nicodemus visited Jesus and asked about salvation. It is in the context of this discussion that Jesus declares, "For God so loved the world that he gave his one and only Son, that whoever believes in him shall not perish but have eternal life." (John 3:16) The heart of the Father is that every person would come to know him and that no one would be lost.

Truth #2

The Holy Spirit draws people to salvation. Because our hearts are so deceived, without the spiritual work of the Holy Spirit we would be lost forever. Through the prompting of the Spirit we are brought to a place where we can consider Christ. Jesus sends the Holy Spirit to convict people of their need for a savior.

> *When he comes, he will prove the world to be in the wrong about sin and righteousness and judgment: about sin, because people do not believe in me; about righteousness, because I am going to the Father, where you can see me no longer; and about judgment, because the prince of this world now stands condemned.* (John 16:8-11)

Jesus sends the Spirit as well to show all people their need to change and repent. He reminds us that sin has consequences and is not to be trifled with. Calling us to repentance, he invites us to greater faith in Christ.

Truth #3
Everything we need for salvation is available to us through the cross. Jesus was the Lamb of God, sacrificed once and for all—for all sins, of all time, of all people. Jesus cried out, "It is finished," while on the cross. What did he mean by that? The word for finished was a business term that meant "paid in full."

Through the cross, the necessary and final payment for the debt of sinfulness was paid. When someone offends or hurts us, we cry that someone has to pay for that. Jesus paid that price for us on the cross.

Through the cross we were also reconciled with God. We, who at one time were enemies of God, now became his friends. Jesus purchased peace. Jesus' work on the cross made it possible that we could become sons and daughters of God. At the cross, we were adopted into his family becoming brothers and sisters of Christ. (John 1:12)

Jesus' death on the cross brings us justification. We

are now acquitted of our sin and God sees us as not guilty.

Christ's work on the cross also brings us regeneration. It is possible for us to be made new. Sin is no longer destroying us, but we have life in Christ.

Truth #4

We are now in the process of being sanctified, a theological term for becoming more and more like Jesus. The cross declares us righteous, and we are marked for a unique work of God. While we will never be perfect in this life, the Holy Spirit is convicting us and equipping us to become more like Christ.

Truth #5

We can stand firm in the salvation of Christ. Once Christ has come into our life, we can be sure that he will keep and protect us. "Jesus said: 'I give them eternal life, and they shall never perish; no one will snatch them out of my hand.'" (John 10:28) When we come to him, Jesus promises we are forgiven and will have an eternal relationship with God. Sin no longer has to reign over us because we are more than conquerors in him.

Get Dusty

A disciple rejoices in Jesus' work on the cross. Knowing what Jesus has accomplished provides confidence to move from our past, strength to live in light of the cross today and hope for God's work tomorrow. You are now reconciled with God, an adopted child of his in the process of becoming like his son. Take time now to thank him for the power of the cross in your life.

Fixed on the Future

By nature, I am a planner always thinking about getting ready for the future. My wife is a person who always lives in the moment. Without each other, I would miss out on a lot of things today, and she would not be quite as ready for tomorrow. Jesus balanced both. He never missed being fully present in any situation, but challenged people to live well in light of the future.

That future included a time when we would stand before the Father for Judgment.

> *When the Son of Man comes in his glory, and all the angels with him, he will sit on his glorious throne. All the nations will be gathered before him, and he will separate the people one from another as a shepherd separates the sheep from the goats. He will put the sheep on his right and the goats on his left.* (Matthew 25:31-33)

That judgment leads to one of two destinations. One is present with God in heaven and the other is separated from him in hell.

Those who know Christ and who have trusted in his finished work on the cross will experience heaven. "Then the King will say to those on his right, "Come, you who are blessed by my Father; take your inheritance, the kingdom prepared for you since the creation of the world.'" (Matthew 25:34) The Gospels record about 140 references to Heaven. Jesus said that heaven is a real place, and he used different words to describe it. He called it a paradise. He called it rest. He says it is a place of great joy and reward. (Matthew 25) He encouraged the disciples to not be troubled by his leaving because he was going to prepare a mansion for them in heaven. The word mansion is less about a large home and more about a resting place of safety. As the earth was a prepared place for Adam and Eve, Jesus was preparing a new place for us. (John 14:2)

Jesus taught the disciples that the way we live our life here on earth has an effect on our life in heaven. We should be storing up treasures in heaven instead of here on earth. To only invest in this world is the ultimate waste. Our time and investment should be in things that last. (Matthew 6:20) Jesus urged us to use our treasure here to gain friends who will greet us in heaven. (Luke 16:9)

Jesus encouraged us to pray that God's will would be done here on earth as it is in heaven. (Matthew 6:10) We should pray that as God reigns and rules there, that he does so on earth as well. Our prayer life deepens as we study what heaven is like to know how to pray effectively here.

Not everyone will be in heaven, though. Heaven is a place of justice. God judges people justly, and their reward is appropriate. (Luke 16) Jesus taught about a time of judgment when an account would be given. Those in Christ would enter the joy of heaven. Those who have disregarded Christ would be eternally separated from him. "Then he will say to those on his left, 'Depart from me, you who are cursed, into the eternal fire prepared for the devil and his angels.'" *(Matthew 25:41)* What we choose in this life affects the next life.

Jesus taught, too, that hell was a real place. He described it as a place of eternal fire and of eternal punishment with no rest. (Matthew 5:22) Jesus also speaks of it as a garbage dump and a place of weeping and gnashing of teeth. Jesus is saying that in hell nothing can satisfy your souls. There will be such sorrow and weeping and longing that nothing can satisfy. Imagine a person is there, completely cut off by God, but they did not want to surrender to him in this life. You are therefore separated from the one person who has the power to satisfy your soul.

While the idea of hell is repugnant to many, hell reveals to us the holiness of God. Hell is hell because God is God. Were there no hell, then God would have nothing to show he is just. Hell shows us God is serious about judging sin.

Get Dusty

Despite our circumstances, a disciple lives every day with hope knowing that heaven is coming. While we may struggle in this life, our few short years here are nothing compared to an eternity with him. Knowing that either hell or heaven is a person's destiny, we should be motivated to populate heaven with as many people as we can. Today, who do you know whose life hangs in the balance of eternity? Who needs to know about the love of Jesus and the hope of heaven? Share Jesus with them.

Character-Driven

Perhaps one of the best definitions I have heard of character is that it is who you really are and what you do when no one is looking. It is the true you that you know yourself to be. Those disciples who followed Jesus saw this in him. The person he was in front of people was the person he was in the private moments when no one was looking. And if you are looking for what that character might be, the best place to start is with the fruit of the Spirit which Paul writes about in Galatians 5:22-23.

Closely following Jesus, the disciples saw him bear fruit every day. They saw his love for children, the sinner and the outcast. They saw his joy when the 70 returned having been sent out and he was elated with what they had done. They saw his peace in the midst of storms and difficulty. They saw his patience when people falsely accused him. They saw his kindness in the gentle way he touched and healed people. They saw him as the good shepherd who gave his life for his sheep. They saw his faithfulness in his resolve to do what the Father had asked him to do. They saw his self-control when on the cross he surrendered to the Father instead of lashing out.

The disciples heard Jesus consistently teaching about
42

repentance, the turning away from the old life of sin toward a new life of pursuing Christ. (Matthew 4:17) Paul describes this as putting off the old way of life and putting on a new way of life. Repentance says, "I don't want to live as I did anymore, and I am walking away from that to live a new life." The Holy Spirit, in his grace and mercy, reveals those sinful areas in our life and invites us to turn from that toward Christ. Knowing the importance of repentance, a disciple intentionally turns away from sin to put on the holiness of Christ.

Get Dusty

When you review the fruit of the Spirit, does the Holy Spirit prompt you with one of those that could use some attention in your life? Have there been times when you have not walked in that character trait? Maybe there is even someone you should apologize to. You can lie to others about these, but you can't fool God. Funny how we want him to see us when we are in need or pain, but there are times when we hope He doesn't see the sin our life. Maybe you want to confess to God that you didn't walk in his peace, you rejected his love or chose not to be faithful to him.

A disciple follows the master in living out the eight

character traits from Galatians 5 when people are watching *and* when only the Father is looking. Each day, pray for a different fruit of the Spirit. You might want to pray for love every day and then for different trait each of the seven days of the week. May the dust of Christ's character cover you.

Spiritually-Disciplined

But Jesus often withdrew to lonely places and prayed.
(Luke 5:15)

This is a short verse packed with life-giving truth. If you had been following Jesus while he was on earth, you would have seen him intentionally moving away from all the competing voices to be alone with the Father. The disciples witnessed the importance Jesus placed on developing his relationship with the Father. I know it raises questions. As part of the Trinity, was Jesus praying to himself when he prayed? If he was God, did he even need to pray?

Throughout the gospels, Jesus adhered to disciplines in his life to intentionally cultivate his relationship with the Father. These are important disciplines for all followers of Christ.

- Worship: Jesus regularly worshipped in the synagogues and temple.
- Fasting: He spent 40 days fasting and praying in the wilderness.
- Thanksgiving: In his darkest moments, he broke bread and gave thanks.
- Surrender: At every turn, he surrendered his life to the will of the Father.

- Learning: As a young boy, he committed to learning and growing.
- Rest: At the end of busy days, he would find time to rest—at least once in the bottom of a boat.

Jesus structured his life so all these could happen. These are the disciplines of a disciple. While not daily activities, a dusty disciple creates rhythms in their life to nurture their spirit and to inspire others to want to care for their souls. The disciples witnessed Jesus' prayer life and wanted to imitate it. Later on, the early church saw the spiritual life of Peter, James, John and others who gathered together to learn how to imitate them.

Get Dusty

How does a disciple grow in these many areas? When I see someone whose spiritual life inspires me, I become the most intrusive person imaginable. I seek to get as close to them as possible so I can to learn how they pray, how they fast, how they worship, how they listen and how they seek God. Find someone whose spiritual life inspires you. Spend some time with them, asking particularly about the disciplines they have for their spiritual life.

Family-Oriented

One of the great mysteries of the faith is that we worship one God in three persons. The Father, Son and Holy Spirit exist as three persons in one God. From the beginning God has never been alone, and this is likely why God said it was not a good thing for Adam to be alone. God called out Abraham to create a people for himself, and then God called a nation to bear the light of his goodness. It comes as no surprise that rarely do we see Jesus alone. He formed deep relationships with people. They traveled together, ate together, celebrated together and worshipped together. Although Jesus was alone in the wilderness when he was tempted and alone with the Father in times of prayer, most of his time was spent in the company of his disciples.

The gospels infer that within that group, Jesus had some unique relationships. When Jesus met with Elijah and Moses on the Mount of Transfiguration, only Peter, James and John were with him. They alone got to witness something unique. (Matthew 17, Luke 9) Even within that three, John intimates that his relationship with Jesus was different than the others as he refers to himself as the disciple Jesus loved the most. (John 19:26)

Those following Jesus saw that he lived in close relationship with other people. This is not always a popular concept in twentieth century America. In our world of rugged individualism, we resist the whole idea of living in community, fearing it smacks of communism or of hippie life in the 1960s. How the early Christians lived in community together seemed to evolve and shift from place to place, but suffice it to say that a disciple can't follow Jesus and yet claim to not to need to be around Christians. The only true way we reflect what God is like is to reflect his relational love.

I'll be the first to admit this is not easy. In fact, it is hard work dealing with our differences and trying to find common ground. The twelve disciples didn't live in an idyllic brotherhood either. Simon the Zealot hated the Romans and gave his life trying to thwart Roman rule. Matthew the Tax Collector threw away his integrity to collect taxes to benefit that same Roman government. These two men, who had every reason to hate each other, found common grace at the feet of Jesus. I am sure, though, that they had some challenging conversations. I can only imagine the eye rolls of some disciples when Peter opened his mouth. John was known as the Son of Thunder, and his bombastic nature surely offended some in the group.

Within the church, very different people are all trying to follow Jesus together. Sometimes it seems that it would be easier to avoid people instead of getting together. Dusty disciples don't avoid people, they seek out one another. They know Satan wants us to isolate, but Jesus wants us to love, serve, encourage, support and care for one another. Dusty disciples worship together, enjoying the presence of God in corporate worship. They find time to meet with a small group of other believers who share the dust and help nurture the soul. If you are not part of a small group or don't have a couple Christians you meet with regularly, seek out a small group or find someone who will come near and disciple you.

Get Dusty

Regular worship with your church family is vitally important. Make a commitment to worship every weekend. If you are not part of a small group, then consider being part of one. If you are going through this material with another disciple, thank them for their investment of time in your life. If you are not walking through this with another person, you are missing out on some rich discussions. Invite another person to share this journey with you.

Servant-Devoted

Near the end of his earthly ministry, James and John took Jesus aside and asked if they could have a privileged place next to him. Others heard their conversation and weren't too happy with the brothers. Jesus, though, responded with a challenge to the bickering and power-hungry brothers:

> *.... whoever wants to become great among you must be your servant, and whoever wants to be first must be slave of all. For even the Son of Man did not come to be served, but to serve, and to give his life as a ransom for many. (John 10:44-45)*

Paul also reminds us in Philippians 2 that Jesus emptied himself of all his glory and became as a servant, obedient to even death on a cross. The night before he was betrayed, Jesus took off his robe, picked up a basin and washed the feet of the disciples because there was no household servant to do that. He served the hungry by providing food. He served the sick by offering healing. He served the outcast by giving them dignity.

More than serving though, he was a servant. Those are two different things. We can all serve from time to time. There is a need and we meet it. It makes us feel good when we choose to serve. However, the disciples saw that Jesus did not serve only when it was convenient or when it made him look good. At his core, Jesus was a servant. He served when He did not have a choice. He served because it was his nature. He served when it wasn't even to his advantage.

The disciples had trouble serving one another while Jesus was alive, but after his resurrection, they changed and developed a completely different attitude. It was this servant attitude that catapulted the church into a major movement. Christian disciples did the most inexplicable things. They sacrificed money for the poor. They fed the widows. They cared for the orphan. They ministered to the sick during deadly epidemics when everyone else, including the doctors, had left town. The gospel continues to advance in places where Christ-followers humble themselves and serve.

I am not sure what Jesus would have thought of modern day churches that invite people to come to Jesus in hopes of achieving greater wealth and success. It is not what he modeled. There is nothing in the gospel about worldly self-advancement. Rather Paul urges us to have the same attitude as Jesus and become a servant. Disciples are dusty servants, eager to put the needs of others at the top of their agenda.

Get Dusty

If you ask Jesus who you can serve, I am sure he will bring someone to mind. Ask them how you can serve. Find some time to do that. Jesus wrapped a towel around himself and got dirty. You will never feel more like him than when that towel is around your waist.

Kingdom-Minded

Jesus balanced several missional activities at the same time, including sharing the gospel and discipling twelve future leaders. He was also devoted to the largest building project ever attempted on planet earth, and he invites you to join him.

In the small community of Caesarea Philippi, surrounded by several pagan temples, Jesus first announced it. To Peter, who had just proclaimed that Jesus was indeed the Christ, Jesus said: "I tell you that you are Peter, and on this rock I will build my church, and the gates of Hades will not overcome it." (Matthew 16:18) The disciples watched him give his life to building the church and they followed suit.

The church simply refers to the called-out ones— people called out to build something different from everyone else. We are all natural-born builders. Most of the time we are building our own little kingdoms where we are the king or queen. We want our kingdom of financial security, guaranteed happiness, minimal conflict, personal success and recognition. We want a kingdom where everything is under our control and nothing happens that catches us off guard. We want a faith-free kingdom. That is not, however, what he is building. The twelve disciples gave up creating their own little kingdom for the challenge of building his. They gave up security for a life of faith. They invested in a kingdom that would last. This was incredibly ambitious. This was visionary. This would require faith.

This king, Jesus, called his disciples and calls us to a much grander vision of a kingdom. He calls us to the pursuit of something greater than ourselves that will outlast us and have an eternal impact. Build his church. Advance his kingdom.

Why is the church suffering today? Why are people unimpressed with the whole concept? We have simply stopped building the church the way Jesus directed. We have stopped pursuing the kingdom. Instead, we invite Jesus to lend his hand to the building of our kingdoms. If we can have a little bit of Jesus, it might make our kingdoms better. There is nothing inspiring about that.

To be honest I struggle with this every day. I like my kingdoms. I like my control. I like to invite Jesus to make my life a little bit better. But I live with a new allegiance not to me, but to him; a life that is not my own, but to live as Christ lived for his kingdom. A disciple chooses every day to stop laying the bricks of his own kingdom and to build the church of Jesus.

Get Dusty

Jesus taught us to pray, "Your kingdom come." You have probably been praying more about your kingdom than his. Lay your kingdom down at the foot of the cross right now. Pray that his kingdom would advance in your life.

Conclusion

As they followed Jesus, the disciples developed the mind of Christ that led their lives into action. A disciple has the head of Christ living as he lived. Paul wrote to the church in Rome encouraging them to let God and his word continually renew their own mind. (Romans 12:1-3)

As you review this chapter, what thoughts does God need to renew for you?

Ask God to give you the mind of Christ. Take out your calendar and schedule new routines with him. Deepen your connection with other Christians. Serve someone today because you are a servant. Commit to putting off some old habits and putting on new ones.

CHAPTER 2

HEART - The Emotions of Jesus

I spent the summer of 1981 as a researcher for one of my university professors. He was writing a book on social and political rebellion in early Canada and was paying me to pour through old texts and historical archives to gather information. It was a great job giving me flexible hours and a summer spent reading, but my first few weeks were miserable. I was sifting through massive amounts of material organizing it in a way I thought was most beneficial for his writing; but he was disappointed with my results. He knew that I had worked hard, but I had worked hard in a way that was of no help to him. Were I to write a book, the material was perfect. It just wasn't his style. While I had studied with this professor for a couple years, now I needed to study him. I had to study what motivated him, what drove his thought process, what excited him and what made him who he was. I had to anticipate what information was important and necessary to help him write the book. Once I got inside his head and took on his identity, the summer project went so much better.

The disciples following Jesus had a similar challenge. Yes, they could live as Jesus lived. They could structure their lives to be gospel-centered, spiritually-disciplined and kingdom-minded. That is not all that is required of a disciple. A disciple is more than a mimic. Jesus wanted his disciples to live authentically out of the new reality of who they were. Doing the right things had to come from the best place. They were not merely to duplicate his actions, but to live out of a new identity.

The oft missing, yet critically important aspect of discipleship is learning to live out of our true identity. Do we have the heart of Christ? While you may say this is a thinking and knowing issue, it is also very much a heart and emotion issue.

Over the years churches have aligned or divided on having the right truths or doctrines. We call that orthodoxy. Orthodoxy pursues the right beliefs making sure that one's beliefs about God, salvation and the church are what the Bible teaches. Christians align and divide over what truths are "right."

Orthopraxy pursues right actions. When people believe the right things, it is assumed they will do the right things. Orthopraxy asks if my actions align with scripture.

Please understand these two are extremely important. We are what we think, but we are also what we feel. Rarely do churches talk about orthopathy.

Orthopathy is having the right feelings about things. Am I feeling as I should? Do I share the "right" beliefs and do the "right" things from the depths of what feels "right" in my heart? I realize how difficult that is and that our feelings cannot always be trusted. We can put a smile on our face and say or do just about anything, but hate it on the inside. Although sometimes that is the best decision, long to live authentically feeling what they believe and do.

The stumbling block many followers of Jesus have is that their feelings get in the way of what they believe to be true. I don't know how many times I have heard people say (including myself), "I just don't feel like doing that!" God wants me happy and being obedient isn't making me happy. When people walk away from Christ and faith, usually it is not because they have changed their mind about something, it is because their feelings are driving them in a particular direction.

In order to become true disciples of Jesus, we have to evaluate our emotions in light of our identity. Jesus showed us how to do that. He had such a deep and abiding sense of who He was. He walked in his identity and authority as the Son of God. He knew where he came from, who he truly was and the influence that he could wield. He was not a robot simply going through the appropriate motions. He was the living expression of God's identity for us. A disciple then, wants to get covered in the dust of the emotions and identity of his teacher. While this discussion could be endless, we'll examine seven truths about our identity and emotions over the next week.

Loved by the Father

The verses that bring me to tears are those that speak of the Father's deep love for his son. At the beginning of his ministry, Jesus surrenders to John's baptism of repentance. In that moment, the heavens crack open and the Father proudly announces his love for the son. "And a voice from heaven said, 'This is my Son, whom I love; with him I am well pleased.'" (Matthew 3:17)

Public pronouncements of deep feelings are life-giving. A similar event happens near the end of his ministry on the Mount of Transfiguration. Jesus takes James, John and Peter to the top of a mountain, reveals his glory, and the sky splits apart again. In that moment the Father says again, "This is my Son, whom I love. Listen to him!" *(Mark 9:7)* The disciples saw firsthand what it is like to rest in the love of the Father. Doing the will of the Father and speaking the words of the Father were the natural outflow of the security of being loved by the Father. Because Jesus rested in that love, verbal attacks on his character and origin did not bother him. Being falsely accused and betrayed did not faze him. Stooping down to wash feet was not beneath him. He was secure in who he was.

We are loved by God more than we can imagine.

- He knows the hairs on your head. (Luke 12:7)
- Your name is tattooed on his hand. (Isaiah 49:16)
- He knows the numbers of your days. (Psalm 139:16)
- He holds your tears in a bottle. (Psalm 56:8)
- Jesus laid down his life for us while we were still entangled in sin. (John 3:16)

Disciples choose to live out of that love, even when feeling that love is a struggle. We have to remind ourselves every day. It might mean taking up the cross and putting to death the self-doubts and self-hatred we have. The Father loves you completely. Let that be enough. Hear those same words spoken to you. You are my child, whom I love.

Get Dusty

Remind yourself now how much the Father loves you. The next time you feel alone, tell yourself how loved you really are. If a co-worker criticizes you, tell yourself how loved you are. Write it in a conspicuous place where you will see it every day. When those feelings of self-doubt creep in, shout at the top of your lungs, "The Father loves me!" Don't just tell yourself you are loved. Live it.

Lover of Others

When we are securely loved, we can become lovers ourselves. Jesus did not simply revel in the Father's love, he shared it liberally. Following Jesus closely, the disciples could not miss the radical and transformative way he loved others. Love changes people.

- They watched him stop dead in his tracks because a woman did not accidentally bump into him, but intentionally reached out for him. She left that encounter healed.
- They watched him lock eyes with a loner named, Zacchaeus, and invite himself for dinner. Zacchaeus finished up dessert as a changed man.
- They watched the most hardened prostitutes, tax collectors and sinners soften when they hung out with Jesus.
- They knew humility and servitude as they watched him wash away the mud caked on their feet.

There was no sense that Jesus did any of this out of obligation or to make himself look good. He was a lover of souls. It was his core identity. He could not *not love people*. He looked beyond the differences and brokenness of people to find any vestige of image of God within them, and then he poured his love into them. The more he loved, the more whole that image became. God is love.

Because loving others was at the heart of Jesus' life and teaching, so it has to be at the heart of a disciple. When he was asked to sum up all the Old Testament laws, "He answered, 'Love the Lord your God with all your heart and with all your soul and with all your strength and with all your mind;' and, 'love your neighbor as yourself.'" (Luke 10:27) A disciple loves when people in need come to them. A disciple looks for opportunities to love. A disciple loves those the world struggles to love because that is what Jesus did. Disciples cannot *not love*.

Being a lover of people is a daunting task. How is one person supposed to love seven billion on the planet? With his disciples listening, Jesus spoke of a journey down the dangerous road to Jericho. On that road, a Samaritan encountered a wounded soul. Knowing it was a dangerous road, there could have been other wounded people on the road. There were other people needing love in his life, but this man started with one. While not everyone experienced the full force of Jesus' love firsthand, they knew without a doubt that he is love. A disciple rests in God's love and distributes the love they have received to another who needs it. Who needs that love today?

Get Dusty

Who in your crowd needs a reminder that they are loved by the Father just as you are? It might be your family, a coworker, a friend, a small group member or even a stranger. Practice a random act of kindness letting that person know today they are loved more than they could ever know.

New in Christ

The anticipation that something new was about to happen was part of what compelled the disciples to follow Jesus. They wanted to be a part of it! As they followed him, a word kept recurring in his teaching. It was the word "new."

He gave a new command: "A **new** command I give you: Love one another. As I have loved you, so you must love one another." (John 13:34)

He launched a new covenant: "In the same way, after the supper he took the cup, saying, 'This cup is the **new** covenant in my blood, which is poured out for you.'" (Luke 22:20)

He empowered them to live new lives: "He told them this parable: 'No one tears a piece out of a **new** garment to patch an old one. Otherwise, they will have torn the **new** garment, and the patch from the **new** will not match the old.'" (Luke 5:36)

It was never business as usual with Jesus or the same old, same old. Jesus was doing a new thing, and the disciples had a front row seat. He was not doing the same things other rabbis had done; he was shaking things up. When He ascended, the disciples launched a brand-new movement because they were brand new people. They began to think and feel as He did to continue his new work.

When you become a follower of Christ, you become a brand-new person. Being a disciple is not a little fixer-upper project with just a few repairs on our life; we are becoming completely new people. We have a new master, a new commandment, a new covenant and new hope.

We need a new mind to think of Christ as He truly is.
We need a new heart to love unconditionally as He loves.
We need a new motivation to live.
We were spiritually dead but now we are alive.
We were enemies of God, but now we are friends.
We were slaves to sin, but now we have a new master!

We are not who we were. We are not what we used to be. We aren't what people say we are. We are not what the enemy accuses us of being. We are made new. The old is passed away. Disciples approach the Father knowing he does not see who we used to be, but knowing that he sees us new in Christ.

Get Dusty

Ask Jesus today to do something new in your life, to break you free from your past and to fill you with a fresh wind of his Spirit. Take up that cross and put to death the reminders of the old you. If you have never been baptized, make a commitment to do that. It is an outward expression that you have been washed new.

Forgiven

I've beaten myself up on many occasions, wondering why I said something or did something. At times, I look at my wife wondering how she can forgive me for something when I still feel so much regret. A disciple walks free in the forgiveness of Christ. We are not truly free if guilt weighs us down. The prison most difficult to break free from is guilt.

The disciples would not have been able to see Jesus walking in forgiveness. Having never sinned, he never needed forgiveness. But seeing him in action for a few moments made them realize he wanted others to walk in forgiveness. This, of course, infuriated his religious contemporaries. Who was he to offer forgiveness? He was God. Odd isn't it, that good people wanted everyone else to live in the bondage of guilt. Jesus made sure that humble, broken and repentant people received forgiveness.

- A Samaritan woman passed from husband to husband found forgiveness, hope and purpose in Jesus. (John 4)

- A man desperate to have Jesus help him walk, was lowered by his friends through a hole in a roof to the place where Jesus was teaching. That man learned his greatest need was not strong legs; his greatest need was a clean conscience. Jesus forgave him. (Mark 2:1-12)

- A half-naked woman pushed around by some hypocritical men found forgiveness in Jesus. When her accusers left, Jesus said he did not condemn her and declared, "Go now and leave your life of sin." (John 8:11c)

- During his last moments on a cross, when one petty thief defended him to another, Jesus pushed through his own agony to make sure that the thief knew he had forgiveness and life.

Jesus wanted every person he encountered to leave with full forgiveness and to share that forgiveness with others. The apostle Peter is a great example of this. Having abandoned Jesus during his hour of need prior to the crucifixion, Peter was riddled with regret. But on a beach after his resurrection, Jesus forgave him. For the rest of his life, Peter walked in forgiveness and victory.

It can be difficult to forgive others, but the hardest person to forgive is often ourselves. It's a popular axiom, but the truth is that we don't need to forgive ourselves. We need to lay down our burden of guilt. If the savior forgives you, you are forgiven. If the creator of the world forgives you, then you are forgiven.

This is now our identity. We are forgiven. What guilt weighs you down? What do you keep beating yourself up about? Jesus paid the price for our sin and shame by taking a beating on the cross. He was beaten so that we don't have to beat ourselves up. When we confess our sins, Jesus is faithful to forgive and to cleanse us from the effects of sin around us. (John 1:8)

Paul lived powerfully knowing he was forgiven. He had been a murderous threat to Christianity. Then he became an apostle. Think of the process he must have gone through to experience the peace of forgiveness. He wanted Christ-followers in Rome to know the same thing. Paul wrote, "Therefore, there is now no condemnation for those who are in Christ Jesus." (Romans 8:1)

Get Dusty

Most people I know struggle with thoughts of self-condemnation and guilt. If Paul struggled, you can bet you will too. If you are feeling condemnation for something you continue to do, then surrender that to Jesus and seek accountability to change. If you feel condemnation for something you have done from the past, then the cross has taken care of that. God no longer sees you as you were, but sees you in Christ. Lay that guilt burden down at the foot of the cross. Now go and get someone dusty with that same truth.

Forgiver

The twelve disciples learned from their rabbi, Jesus, that forgiven people become forgivers. The power of forgiveness has changed you when you are able to lavish forgiveness toward others.

In Matthew 18, Jesus tells the story of a servant who owed his master a tremendous amount of money that he was unable to pay. The king forgave the debt. That same servant later encountered someone who owed him a very tiny amount of money. Instead of forgiving the debt, he threw the servant in prison. Everything changed when the master got word of that.

> *Then the master called the servant in. "You wicked servant," he said, "I canceled all that debt of yours because you begged me to. Shouldn't you have had mercy on your fellow servant just as I had on you?" In anger his master handed him over to the jailers to be tortured, until he should pay back all he owed. "This is how my heavenly Father will treat each of you unless you forgive your brother or sister from your heart."*
> *(Matthew 18:32-35)*

It seemed impossible to the master that someone who had been forgiven so much would withhold forgiveness over something minor. When all our brokenness and sin has been made right at the cross, it makes no sense to hold on to the petty grudges we may have. Jesus said we should make that part of our prayer life, asking for forgiveness as we forgive others. It makes no sense to plead for forgiveness when we can't forgive. Forgiven people become forgivers.

Disciples are forgivers. It is who we are. Out of the lavish freedom of being forgiven, we forgive. Forgiveness does not mean that the person's actions were not wrong. It does not mean that they are off the hook. It does not mean that what they did not affect us. Rather, forgiveness means we don't stand around anymore waiting for them to apologize or admit that they were wrong. When we have been hurt, we want someone to pay. We want the other to experience the pain we experience, however any price they could pay is probably not sufficient anyway. Forgiveness is cancelling my demand that they do or say anything.

Forgiveness does not mean that we trust them completely again. Trust takes time to be rebuilt. It doesn't mean we go back to the way things always were. It means they no longer owe us anything. The debt has been cancelled just like our spiritual debt with the Father is cancelled.

Get Dusty

Do people see you as a forgiver? Jesus was a forgiver and those who follow him live that identity now too. Practice forgiveness. Grow that part of you. Go through the day intentionally forgiving even the little hurts that come. When forgiving another is difficult, focus less on your pain and on the lavish love of the Father. Start today. Remind yourself of the debts you have been forgiven of and then pass that grace around.

Citizen of Heaven

I am sure the disciples had many head-scratching conversations trying to sort out exactly what Jesus meant at times. One of those occasions had to have been when Jesus talked about not being of this world. "But he continued, 'You are from below; I am from above. You are of this world; I am not of this world.'" (John 8:23) "Jesus said, 'My kingdom is not of this world. If it were, my servants would fight to prevent my arrest by the Jewish leaders. But now my kingdom is from another place.'" (John 18:36)

The disciples noticed that Jesus was not gripped by the things of this world. He was not tied to material possessions, fame did not motivate him, nor did he seek to please. He was certainly impacted by things in this world such as poverty, famine, suffering, and legalism but he did not allow them to dominate him. He walked in the power of the Spirit. He lived by the laws of this world, but he was not controlled by them.

Knowing that his true citizenship was not of this world, but of heaven, he was able to say a resounding "no" to the things this world offers.

He said no to people pleasing and yes to

honoring God.

He said no to the shortcuts of sin and yes to obedience God's way.

He said no to pleasing people and yes to pleasing God.

He said no to riches and pleasures of this world and yes to the pleasure of the Father.

He said no to me-first, front-of-the-line mentality and a yes to servant of many.

He said 'no' to using people and loving money so he could say yes to God.

He said no to the consumerism of the moment and a yes for living in light of heaven.

He said no to the powers of the world and yes to the authority of God.

He said no to being of the world, so He could say a resounding yes to influencing it.

The disciples modeled to the church a life unattached from this world. They did not build homes, edifices and careers for themselves. Instead, they said a joyful no to the trappings of this world. Many were willing to suffer persecution because of their hope of heaven.

This is not easy for us. We find ourselves so much a part of this world that it is easy to get caught up in things. However, Paul wrote: "But our citizenship is in heaven. And we eagerly await a Savior from there, the Lord Jesus Christ." (Philippians 3:20) While we may walk in this world, it is not our home. Our true home is in heaven. We were not meant for this life forever; instead we should be eagerly awaiting a different way of living.

Get Dusty

Disciples know how to say "yes" to the things that matter and "no" to what doesn't. Disciples are no longer world-consumers, but kingdom-contributors. This is so countercultural. Today you are a citizen of heaven. Study heaven. Contemplate heaven. Pray that what happens there would happen here. Do one thing that will store up treasure in heaven right now. Use your resources to make sure as many people get there as possible.

Steward of God's Riches

Money dominates much of what we do. We earn it, spend it, save it, crave it, think about it, worry about it, and manipulate with it. From the time we are born, we have an ownership identity. Think of the some of the first words out of a toddler's mouth, and I'll bet that the word "mine" is at the top of the list. But that ownership identity is no longer yours if you have decided to follow Jesus. You have a new one that even applies to money, time and your other resources. Jesus talked more about money than most other topics, because he knew the pull it has on this world and how difficult it would be to live out of our true citizenship if we try hold on to it. Our hearts always follow our treasure and a disciple understands where their true treasure is.

Jesus' teaching on money was relatively simple. Over and over the disciples listened as Jesus taught stories that reflected God as the king or business owner and his people as stewards or managers. (John 25:14-30) He taught stewardship over ownership. God owns our stuff and we manage it.

Let that sink in for a moment.

You are no longer the owner of your stuff. God owns

it. That thought is more than enough to give us pause. At first that may be shocking, but it is highly liberating. He owns it. You are the steward or manager. Now let's manage it knowing one day we will stand before him to give an account of how well we did.

As a manager, the Bible gives us some principles of wealth.

- Earn money ethically. Money itself is not a bad thing. It is the love of money that is a problem. Earn money in a way that honors God.

- Give the first of it to God. Jesus taught the principle of being generous to God. We give the first part of our time and the first part of our resources. (Luke 6:38, Malachi 3:10)

- Save some for the future. Proverbs speaks about making sure that we store up some money for the future. We don't have to hoard huge amounts, but wisely prepare for the future. (Proverbs 21:20)

- Live off the rest. We can rest well when we live off the rest of our resources. When we trust him with that, we can be assured he will watch over the rest. After all it is not ours, it is his.

We are also stewards of the spiritual gifts God has given us to make a difference for the kingdom. We don't use our talents and abilities for ourselves, but for the kingdom. (Mark 6:8-11)

We steward the time God has given us. Jesus rested and on the Sabbath, he worshipped and rested as well. As a steward, Jesus made sure that he did not use his time, talents and treasures for himself but for the end goal of God's glory.

> So Jesus said, "When you have lifted up the Son of Man, then you will know that I am he and that I do nothing on my own but speak just what the Father has taught me. The one who sent me is with me; he has not left me alone, for I always do what pleases him." (John 8:28-29)

Get Dusty

Deciding to be a steward changes everything. You can't walk in the love of God and find peace in stuff. You can't rest in the forgiveness of God if you are worried whether you will have enough. You can't reflect heavenly values if you want to store up treasure on earth. You can't live as a new creation giving glory to God if you want stuff to bring you glory. Maybe you need to pick up the cross and put to death the desire to own stuff. You may need to put to death the security you find in stuff instead of in Christ. You may need to put to death the glory of ownership, working instead to bring glory to the Father.

Conclusion

The enemy of our soul knows the power of identity. As a deceiver, he can only deceive. We live our lives based on our identity. For that reason, he does not want us to live out or even know our destiny. If we believe we are worthless, we treat ourselves as such. If we believe we are unloved, we will look for love in all the wrong places. If we believe in our own importance, we will never pick up a cross and die to ourselves. If we believe we are owners rather than stewards, we will never learn to be generous and manage our time, talents and resources for God's glory.

Which of these identities do you most struggle to live out? Pick one. Pray each day about it. Study verses that speak to its truth. Formulate a new set of actions based on what you have learned. Study to see how Jesus lived out that identity. But remember this, we cannot possibly live out of this identity on our own. It takes all the resources of heaven and the Holy Spirit living inside us for those changes to take place. The good thing is, God gives those resources and the Holy Spirit freely to all who are willing to develop the heart of Christ.

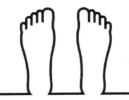

CHAPTER 3

FEET - Standing Firm as Jesus Did

But I tried and I just can't do it!

I have said those words countless times. I've worked hard to make real changes in my life, failed, then tried harder and then my hardest to get the results that I want. Still, I fail.

People share words like this with me in moments of spiritual frustration. They've tried hard to follow the Bible. They tried hard to live like Jesus. They tried hard to be spiritual, but in their trying, they failed.

You may be saying those words to yourself as you get to this point in the journey of discipleship. I have tried to live like Jesus and feel like him, but it has not worked for me. I think the biggest misconception people have about Christianity is that it is a religion of self-help. Follow these four steps to happiness and these eight principles for joy and these five ways to live and life will get better. If those attempts don't work out, it means you haven't put the work in you need to and you'll just have to try harder.

The disciples knew following Jesus was not at all a self-help exercise. They saw that Jesus never did anything solely in his strength; instead, he modeled for them a life that rested on the will of the Father and leaned on the power of the Holy Spirit.

Klaus Issler speaks to this well in his book, <u>Living into the Life of Jesus: The Formation of Christian Character</u>, in which he examines using Jesus as a role model for spiritual growth. Of course, some see a problem with that. Since we are so vastly different from Jesus who was not only fully human, but fully God, how can we possibly grow spiritually as He did? Issler likens it to Clark Kent and Superman. What good would it be to try to imitate Clark Kent if Clark was solving all his problems as Superman? We can't turn ourselves into Superman!

Issler argues that we can follow Jesus precisely because he was not Superman or even superhuman. He depended on the resources God had given him through the Trinity. "Jesus predominantly relied on the divine resources of the Father and the Holy Spirit to accomplish his messianic mission." (p110) As he leaned on the Father and the Holy Spirit, so we too can lean on them.

Jesus' teaching, miracles and work were not a result of him being God. He lived a human life empowered by the Holy Spirit in obedience to the Father. What percentage of his life did he live in human effort and what percentage was under the power of the Spirit? I'm not sure we will ever know that answer, nor is it is helpful. What we do know is that Jesus took on the humanity that we have and walked in the power of the Spirit.

The disciples never saw Jesus scrambling to try to fix things. They always saw him with feet firmly planted in the resources God gave to him. They watched him listen to the Father. They watched him being led by the Spirit. They watched him victorious in spiritual battles. When life's storms blew in or the enemy came knocking, Jesus stood with feet firmly planted in the strength of the Spirit. When it came time then to launch the church, these twelve disciples lived their lives the same way standing strong in the Holy Spirit's power.

A disciple knows they cannot do anything in their own strength, but must be empowered by the same Spirit that empowered their rabbi. Otherwise discipleship becomes a one big performance contest....who can do more right things better than others! This is what makes being a disciple the ultimate in humility. We can never do it ourselves, but if we stand with our feet firmly planted as his, resting in the Father and leaning on the Spirit, more could be accomplished than we could imagine.

Let's see where Jesus feet take us.

Filled with the Spirit

Luke tells us how Jesus' feet took him from the Jordan River to the wilderness. What looks like a geographical journey was also a spiritual journey. In Luke 3:22, Jesus is *baptized* by John, and the Holy Spirit, in the form of a dove, descends upon him. Chapter 4 opens with Jesus now being *full* of the Holy Spirit and being *led by* the Holy Spirit into the wilderness to experience forty days of temptation. (Luke 4:1) After that period of temptation, something happens. More than being filled with the Holy Spirit, we are told Jesus returned to Galilee in the power of the Spirit, *(Luke 4:14)* He was *empowered* by the Spirit. He stopped in Galilee to preach his first sermon from Isaiah 61 by saying: "The Spirit of the Lord is on me, because he has anointed me..." (Luke 4:18)

The Holy Spirit plays a key role in the ministry of Jesus.

- The Holy Spirit guided Jesus. (Luke 4:1)
- The Holy Spirit anointed him to speak. (Matthew 12:18-21)
- The Holy Spirit empowered him to accomplish miracles. (Luke 6:19)
- The Holy Spirit was present with Christ at

the crucifixion. (Hebrews 9:14)

Jesus bequeathed the Holy Spirit to his disciples following his death. In the Upper Room before his death, Jesus breathes on them and promises the power of the Spirit. About seven weeks later, on the day of Pentecost, the Holy Spirit baptized them and filled them. They taught and performed miracles just like Jesus in the very same power of the Spirit. As disciples now training other disciples, they would have to lean on the power of the Spirit.

Paul states it plainly in Ephesians: "Do not get drunk on wine, which leads to debauchery. Instead, be filled with the Spirit." (Eph 5:18) The Greek word for "being filled" was a nautical term. It spoke of setting the sails on a ship to the best place to catch the wind. A partnership is necessary for a ship to sail. Sailors have to set the sails and the wind has to blow. When one or the other does not happen, the ship stays put. A partnership is also necessary in the disciple's life. A disciple needs to set their sails and needs the wind of the Holy Spirit to blow. As the sails are set, the Holy Spirit has control of the person's life.

Get Dusty

We can't do the filling ourselves, but we can align the sails of our life to let the Spirit have control. Here is what you can do right now.

- Take a cross to anything else in your life that has control except for Jesus. The Spirit cannot fill you if you are filled with something else.

- Open your life in prayer to the Father humbly asking for the Spirit's filling.

- Take the first step in obedience and watch the power of the Spirit help you.

- Thank God for his Spirit's strength and power every day.

Directed by the Spirit

The first thing the Spirit does in Jesus' life is guide him from the Jordan to a period of temptation in the wilderness.

When our family was quite young, I was invited as the speaker to a wonderful group of missionaries in the Czech Republic. My family got to come along on that trip, and before the conference we had a couple days to tour Prague. Normally I would buy a guidebook and try to navigate my way around the city. On the suggestion of a friend though, I hired a personal tour guide for a couple days. She took us all around the city sharing with us its history and cultural evolution. Knowing we had two young children, she would add some stops just to keep them interested. We were pushing strollers and wheelchairs so she knew the easiest ways to get around. She helped us avoid any of the dangerous places and took us to where the food was just right for our family. As a guide, she brought the guide book to life.

The disciples watched Jesus leaning on the Spirit for guidance, and he taught that the Spirit would do the same for them. "But when he, the Spirit of truth, comes, he will guide you into all the truth." (John

16:13) We have a guidebook in the Scripture. God has clearly and accurately given us his direction for our life, but we have also been given a Guide. We have someone who will take that book and help bring the truths to light and to personal application in our life. He will also lead us to make wise decisions and prompt our conscience about things to do or to avoid.

How does the Spirit do this?

- He will remind you of verses or spiritual truths that you need just for the moment. When you are praying for yourself or others, listen to the verses the Spirit brings to your mind. This is why scripture reading and study is so important. It provides a great base from which the Spirit can lead.

- Listen to the echoes of God in your life. There are times the same verse comes up at different times and in different places throughout my week. It may be on the radio, in a book I read, or someone speaking it to me. Listen to those echoes. Often God repeats what he wants us to hear.

- Listen for the Holy Spirit's promptings. When we are tempted toward evil, we call that temptation. What do we call it when the Spirit leads us toward holiness? It is the Spirit's prompting. Listen to those promptings. Evaluate them against God's word. If they don't go against Scripture, act on them.

- Listen to your conscience. We have all had those sick feelings in our gut that something might be wrong. That could be the Spirit leading. Test that against scripture. Seek out advice, and learn to hear God's voice in your life.

There is a word of caution. We assume that God will lead us to a place where there is the no pain, difficulty or suffering. The truth is that sometimes he does lead us to very difficult places. He led Jesus, filled with the Spirit, to the wilderness, but Jesus left empowered by the Spirit. Don't judge whether God is leading you by the circumstances around you. Trust that even when he leads you through difficult circumstances, you will go from being filled to being empowered.

Get Dusty

Schedule some alone time soon. Take a pen and

paper. Reflect on how the Holy Spirit has been leading you. What has he said through promptings, echoes and people? Write down what you are sensing. Pray about that and take it to trusted people. If this is the Spirit's leading, perhaps it is time to follow.

Rooted in Christ

Centered in a small field on my father's farm was a lone apple tree. Its branches were perfect for climbing and its fruit, when fresh, was simultaneously both wonderfully tart and sweet. Every August its branches were laden with more apples than a family could eat or preserve. I never once, though, saw that tree screwing up its bark, squeezing its branches and curling its roots trying and trying and trying to bear fruit. As it abided in the field, its deep roots and large branches produced lots of fruit.

The disciples never witnessed Jesus anxiously trying to accomplish more. He did not travel frantically from place to place, unsure if he could accomplish it all. He abided and rested in the Father. He knew what the Father wanted and he did it. "'My food,'" said Jesus, "'is to do the will of him who sent me and to finish his work.'" (John 4:34) He talked with the Father daily. He prayed when things got tough and when he had big decisions to make. He rested in the peace of the Father during a great storm. In wrestling with his Father over the crucifixion, he surrendered saying "Not my will be done, but yours."

At the end of his ministry, having rested in his father,

Jesus turned now to his disciples and invited them to abide in him. A disciple abides.

> *I am the vine; you are the branches. If you remain in me and I in you, you will bear much fruit; apart from me you can do nothing. If you do not remain in me, you are like a branch that is thrown away and withers; such branches are picked up, thrown into the fire and burned. If you remain in me and my words remain in you, ask whatever you wish, and it will be done for you. This is to my Father's glory, that you bear much fruit, showing yourselves to be my disciples.*
> *(John 15:5-8)*

How do you know you are abiding? Your sustenance comes from him. You are most satisfied in him alone. Instead of digging roots deep into something else, you dig them into him. Instead of letting your soul be nourished by other things, his word is sustaining you. When that happens, your love for God and his word increases. With roots settled in, your love grows. Then fruit that lasts appears, and our love for him grows more fruit. It is fruit that will last and fruit that will point to the love of God.

Get Dusty

How do we dig our roots deep into Christ? The spiritual disciplines we referenced earlier are God-designed to help us abide. Consistently praying, reading God's word, worshipping, celebrating, fasting and surrendering cultivate the soil for abiding. Pick up those practices if you have gotten too busy. Make sure prayer and scripture reading are part of your life. Even memorize a verse or two that are meaningful to you.

The next phases of the journey will teach us how to abide better as we become aware of where God is working and join him there. Through prayer, we become more confident in him, and his word gives us something to dig our roots deep into. As we look to him and his word alone, the steadiness of abiding will produce more fruit than you can imagine.

Discerning of Spiritual Realities

Jesus taught the disciples to discern when and where the kingdom of darkness was active and to stand in victory against the kingdom.

Nowhere is that clearer than when the Spirit led him to the wilderness and Satan tempted him. What he experienced personally in that wilderness is a picture of what his followers will experience. The kingdom of darkness is always trying to oppose what the people of the kingdom of light are doing. Before Christ, we were living in darkness, but Jesus called us out and into the light. "Jesus spoke again to the people, he said, 'I am the light of the world. Whoever follows me will never walk in darkness, but will have the light of life.'" (John 8:12) Jesus taught this discernment of where Satan was at work so that we could avoid it and join God where he is at work.

Our Western world does not readily recognize dark spiritual realities. We want to live as if faith is unopposed, but that is not the truth. We are at war with a sworn enemy who wants to discredit Christ's testimony, discourage every Christ follower and leave disciples feeling defeated. It's imperative in this war, that a disciple clearly discern what is of the kingdom of darkness and what is of the kingdom of light. We are not left alone with this. The Holy Spirit in us helps us discern what is of God and what is not. Jesus taught his disciples the ways the enemy works in our world.

- He is active when our desires do not want to line up with God's plans. When Peter did not want to believe that Jesus would suffer and die. "Jesus turned and looked at his disciples, he rebuked Peter. 'Get behind me, Satan!' he said. 'You do not have in mind the concerns of God, but merely human concerns.'" (Mark 8:33)

- He is active when he creates chaos to bring doubt. During the Last Supper, Jesus warned Peter that he was under spiritual attack. "Simon, Simon, Satan has asked to sift all of you as wheat." (Luke 22:31) Jesus predicted Peter would deny knowing him. Satan wanted this to become the ultimate defeat for one of the most powerful of apostles.

- He is active when we think religious activity is enough to live a godly life. To those Jews following empty religion, Jesus said:

  You belong to your father, the devil, and you want to carry out your father's desires. He was a murderer from the beginning, not holding to the truth, for there is no truth in him. When he lies, he speaks his native language, for he is a liar and the father of lies. Yet because I tell the truth, you do not believe me! (John 8:44)

The clash of kingdoms still exists today. Peter reminded the church: "Be alert and of sober mind. Your enemy the devil prowls around like a roaring lion looking for someone to devour." (I Peter 5:8) He knew from personal experience how important it is to be on guard and to discern the spiritual reality around us. Disciples are aware of Satan's schemes.

Likewise, Paul reminded the Ephesian church not only to be aware, but to be on guard of the spiritual realities around them. "For our struggle is not against flesh and blood, but against the rulers, against the authorities, against the powers of this dark world and against the spiritual forces of evil in the heavenly realms." (Ephesians 6:12)

Often, we fall into two extremes. We either ignore what the devil may be doing, or we focus all our attention on him. Neither extreme is helpful. A disciple must be evaluating where God is at work and where the enemy is lurking.

Get Dusty

How does one become more discerning? Get close to Jesus and to a discerning individual. Watch how they are able to discern where the enemy is. The more you study God's word, the more you will know the lies of the enemy. Look for the fruit of love. Satan can duplicate almost anything, but he cannot duplicate genuine love. Jesus said you know the marks of the enemy because they are destruction. "The thief comes only to steal and kill and destroy; I have come that they may have life, and have it to the full." (John 10:10) If something is stealing, killing or destroying your joy, faith, love or peace, then take up the cross against it and pray that you may be able to rest in the provisions God has given you for that battle. The largest part of the battle is discerning when something is of the enemy or of God.

The rest of the battle comes in standing firm in the spiritual provisions Jesus gave to us.

Victorious in Battle

The disciples not only learned to be spiritually aware, they learned how to stand against the enemy. Jesus was never taken aback by the devil's schemes. He was always prepared and victorious.

- When tempted by Satan, he responded with the truth of the word of God. (Matthew 4:1-11)

- When Satan asked to sift Peter, Jesus prayed for him. (Luke 22:31-32)

- When confronting impossible spiritual situations, Jesus understood both prayer and fasting were required. (Mark 9:29)

- When addressing the demonically-oppressed, Jesus stood firm, faithfully believing the Kingdom of Light would always be victorious. (Mark 5:9-17)

The disciples, having seen Jesus stand firm against the enemy, knew a disciple must also stand firm using the resources God has given. We are not alone in that battle. We are given all the resources we need. Paul reminds us of those.

Therefore put on the full armor of God, so that when the day of evil comes, you may be able to stand your ground, and after you have done everything, to stand. Stand firm then, with the belt of truth buckled around your waist, with the breastplate of righteousness in place, and with your feet fitted with the readiness that comes from the gospel of peace. In addition to all this, take up the shield of faith, with which you can extinguish all the flaming arrows of the evil one. Take the helmet of salvation and the sword of the Spirit, which is the word of God.
(Ephesians 6:13-17)

We have been given spiritual armaments allowing us to stand firm. Let me ask are you using them?

- Does the good news of the gospel cover your head and guide your thinking?
- Do you counter the lies of the enemy with all the truths of God's word?
- Do you know while our righteousness is as filthy rags, the righteousness of Christ covers us?
- Do you know through Jesus you have peace with God and the peace of God?
- Do you know faith in what Jesus has done

will stop every fiery dart of the enemy?

- Do you know the power that is in the word of God? Speak the word of truth and watch the enemy flee.

Get Dusty

What is the armor? In summary, it is the power of the cross. Remember what a disciple has in their hand? It is a cross. Let the cross of Christ work its power in you. While our battles are often with people, Paul reminds us they have a spiritual origin. Where do you sense the enemy working in your life? Every day, put on the armor reminding yourself you have the mind of Christ, you have the peace of Christ, the righteousness of Christ, the faith of Christ, the power of Christ and the truth of Christ.

Devoted in Prayer

Prayer was nothing new for these twelve disciples. They were all raised in a culture of prayer where you stopped three times during the day to pray. But the way they saw Jesus stand firm in prayer inspired them to ask Jesus to teach them how to talk with the Father. In fact, this is the only time the Bible records the disciples asking for something specific. That question prompted what we know as the Lord's Prayer. (Matthew 6:9-13) Using that as a model for prayer along with other teaching, the disciples became students of prayer.

- Jesus taught them that prayer was like family gathering. Simply put, prayer is conversation with our father. Jesus taught that the greatest challenge in prayer is not the mechanics of prayer, but trusting the one who listens to our prayers. Jesus reminded us that the Creator God, the mighty king of the universe is also a tender father who listens eagerly to the prayers of his children.

- He taught them to pray about everyday needs and activities. They were to ask for their daily bread. They prayed for the coming of the kingdom, but also for the needs of every day. Jesus rose early in the morning to pray for his day (Mark 1:35) and for direction in making significant decisions including who would be the twelve who followed him. (Luke 6:12) Keep a list of answers to prayer as fuel to pray even more.

- He taught them there was power in praying with others. A small group of people who agree with each other in prayer have the powerful presence of Jesus. (Matthew 18:20)

- He taught them to pray privately. While people would publicly stand in the street and pray or while they were in the temple, Jesus said there are times to go into a room, close the door and pray. Prayer is not a way to impress others or to make yourself look good. It reveals our dependence upon the Father. Instead of talking to others first about our situation, we go straight to God. (Matthew 6:6)

- He taught them to be fearless in prayer. Jesus shared an illustration of a man who knocked on his neighbor's door in the middle of the night shamelessly asking for some food. (Luke 11:5-8) In the same way, God wants us to be as bold in our prayers as when the disciples witnessed Jesus fearlessly pray to still a storm, to heal the sick and to multiply food.

- He taught persistence in prayer. Prayer is not only to bring results, but to mature our relationship with God. Conversation in any relationship always deepens the connection. The end result of prayer should be that we know God better. To remind us that the answers are not always instant, but we need to persevere in prayer, he shared an illustration of a widow who needed justice and kept begging a judge to help her. (Luke 18:1-8)

- He taught them to pray in his name. A person's name was a reflection of their character. To pray in the name of Jesus means we ask only for things that are within the character or will of God. Prayers of greed or avarice would not be within his character. The Lord's Prayer reminds us to pray that his will be done, that his would be the glory and that our prayers would not lead us into temptation. The goal of our prayer is not to glorify us, but to honor him. (John 14:13)

There is a tension at times between simply reciting

rote prayers than can become meaningless and then praying only the safe things within our comfort zone. A helpful pattern of prayer I have used is this:

- Adoration and thanksgiving. We approach the Father with praise for who He is and for what He has done. We remember He is our great God.

- Confession: In humility, we confess our sins and shortcomings asking God to hear our prayers from a clean conscience. Jesus taught in the Lord's Prayer that a lack of forgiveness on our part hinders our prayers.

- Surrender: Before we launch into a series of requests, we consciously surrender our lives, agenda and wants to him. This is where we lay our lives down on an altar of sacrifice.

- Requests: We bring our needs, desires and requests to God asking him to provide and do what we cannot.

Get Dusty

Take time to walk through these four elements of prayer. Make sure each of your prayer times have these four elements. Throughout the day make sure you thank God for what He is doing, confess sin even in the moment, lay down your agenda and pray for needs as they arise.

Listener in Prayer

In real life, most of us are better talkers than listeners. The same is true in prayer. When a crisis arises, we rush to prayer asking and demanding God's rescue. Rarely do I hear someone say they are going to meet with God simply to listen. Jesus wanted the disciples to engage as much in listening as he did as they did in talking like he did.

Jesus often spoke of God's relationship with his people as that of a shepherd with their sheep. While the shepherd led, Jesus He talked about the importance of sheep listening to the shepherd. "My sheep listen to my voice; I know them, and they follow me." (John 10:27) Communities would have a communal sheep pen. Various shepherds would bring their flocks to that pen at night for protection and then lead them back to their fields in the morning. The sheep followed the voice of their shepherd because they knew it well.

The disciples knew Jesus listened in prayer. They knew God spoke as they heard God say Jesus was his beloved son. They knew he gave answers to prayer as after praying, Jesus chose the twelve. They saw first-hand the strength God gave to Jesus as he agonized in the Garden of Gethsemane. It may have been this aspect that prompted them to ask to learn more how to pray.

Prayer is not only getting our requests met, it is hearing and following the leading of our good shepherd. The more we abide and listen, the more we will recognize his voice and leading.

- Get around someone you trust who listens and learn from them. Jesus even sent people out in pairs to minister and to pray for others.

- Spend time in the scriptures. The voice of God in the scriptures is the same voice who leads. The more you know the voice of his word, the more clearly you can recognize him. Listening prayer is not to discover new truths or different things about God. Listening prayer is to discover the areas God wants us to apply his truth and word.

- Put yourself in a place where all other voices are eliminated. It is difficult to hear God when so many other voices are competing for our attention. Find a quiet place and set aside some time to listen.

- Write down those things that come to mind.

It may be a person with whom you need to talk. It might be an attitude to change. It could be a passage of scripture to read. His voice might lead you to confess something you had long forgotten but was still lingering.

- Respond to what you have heard. There may be some things to do that you know are right, so do them right away. Other things you might want to test against God's word. You think it is God speaking, but you want to make sure it does not contradict any part of God's word. There may be some things you want to take to other trusted people and ask if they think this is God's leading. Ask them to keep you accountable to be obedient.

Once I became a father, I was amazed how I could pick my crying baby's voice out of a nursery filled with crying babies. A father knows his child's voice. A disciple who listens as Jesus listens, knows his Father's voice.

Get Dusty

Schedule a time away from all the other voices. I know in the busyness of life this is hard. It may be when everyone else is in bed. It may be taking a walk. It might be a long drive. The only agenda for that time is listening. Hear what God may want to say to you.

Intercessor in Prayer

It was not until my mom spent her last six weeks of life wasting away in a hospital that I knew the power of praying for other people. We had cried and we had prayed, and I remember being in a place where I was prayed out. I had spent my life praying for people, but now I didn't know what to pray anymore. When people told us how they prayed on our behalf, it was incredibly life giving. I knew how Moses felt when Aaron and Hur lifted his arms in prayer.

There are times we are asked or feel burdened to pray for someone and to intercede before God on their behalf. This we do in our own prayer rooms or quiet moments. When we feel called to do that:

- We should pray from love. Jesus prayed for people and for difficult things, but he never prayed in a manipulative way. His prayers always came from a heart of love. Our prayer should be that God would do the most loving thing in their lives.

- We pray that God would be glorified in the situation. Jesus was able to minister to people in a way that did not make them or others look good, but that always brought glory to God.

- We pray specifically. We are invited to bring our requests before God—even the smallest details of life, such as our daily bread.

- We pray fervently, and we pray in faith. Jesus said some things need both prayer and fasting. There is a perseverance needed but we pray these things in prayer. I have seen people receive answers to pray, particularly the salvation of family members only after decades of praying. Don't give up. (Mark 9:29)

There are other times we have the privilege of ministering to people in the moment through laying on hands and praying right there with them. We were finishing up our first meeting with a brand new small group by sharing prayer requests and praying for one another. One young woman shared a need, and we spent time praying for her. She began to sob and we wondered what was wrong with our prayer? The tears came because this was the first time anyone had ever prayed for her. Her husband had even been a pastor for a few years, but this was the first time a group of people came and helped carry the burden for her. It moved her.

The disciples saw firsthand the power of praying with people.

- Jesus prayed for the sick and healed them.
- Jesus prayed for the broken and forgave them.
- Jesus prayed for the fearful disciples and calmed them.
- Jesus prayed for provision for the crowd and God multiplied food.
- Jesus prayed that Peter would be protected when Satan wanted to sift him.

People find this intimidating. How do I possibly have something to pray for this person? When given the opportunity to pray for people:

- Pray in the peace of God. People will know how you prayed for them and the spirit in which you shared with them. When the peace of Christ reigns in your life, it will transfer to theirs.

- Pray the power of God's word. Moments like this remind us how important it is to know God's word and to allow God's spirit to bring a word to you. What truth of God's word applies to that situation? What word gives them hope? Pray the fullness of that truth in their life.

- Pray in practicality. We should be willing to be an answer to their prayer if possible. This week my wife was praying for someone and then realized she could be part of that answer. She got up off her knees and went to help that person. Prayer can prompt us to obedience.

God's work is accomplished through prayer. The hardest work of a disciple is to pray.

Get Dusty

Who can you pray for right now? You may want to schedule time to go and pray with them, or you may want to pray for them right where you are. Ask the Father to do his will beyond what we can imagine or think in their lives.

Student of God's Word

There was a time I basically lived off fast food. The decision every day was whether it was McDonald's, Wendy's or Burger King. Fast food is convenient since someone else has chosen it, prepared it and served it up. I just have to digest it. The documentary Supersize Me revealed that you can't live off fast food alone. Now I still enjoy fast food, but I am sustained much more by taking whole foods and creating a healthy meal.

North American Christianity makes spiritual fast food readily available. It is truth from God's word that has been chosen, prepared and served up by someone else. It might be a book, video series or a radio teacher. And yes, we preachers serve up spiritual fast food. We choose the passage, prepare the passage and serve it up to you in church. Now I happen to think my spiritual fast food is pretty good otherwise I wouldn't serve it, but that can't be the only thing a disciple is nourished by. As we have seen, the disciples saw Jesus' commitment to the word.

They knew that from his boyhood Jesus had interacted with the temple priests over the scriptures. (Luke 2:47)

They saw him read the scriptures and claim to fulfill them. (Luke 4:21-22)

They saw people amazed at his knowledge of the scriptures from one who never studied under a rabbi. "The Jews there were amazed and asked, 'How did this man get such learning without having been taught?'" (John 7:15)

Jesus demonstrated the spiritual power of the Word of God in conquering Satan's temptation. Whatever Satan threw at him, Jesus responded with a verse from Deuteronomy. (Luke 4:1-13)

In following Jesus, the disciples knew the importance of the word of God themselves. They were students of the word. Peter's first sermon at Pentecost showed Christ throughout all the Old Testament. Peter and John in their letters refer to Old Testament verses. A disciple certainly learns from teachers, but a disciple knows how to feed themselves.

Studying the scripture is a lifelong pursuit because the more we study, the more we realize there is to study. To get started, here are three activities.

Observation

The Jewish people knew the power of meditating.

This is not the meditation that empties a mind, but the meditation that fills your mind with God's word. Do a little research in a study Bible or online to discover the context of the passage. Who was it written to? Why did the author write it? Read a passage and then read it a few more times. Read it out loud. Look for some key words. What words are repeated? What words stand out? Are there any words that you haven't come across before? Look for cause and effect phrases. Ask yourself the how, why, when, where and what questions. What is the main idea?

Interpretation

Now taking what you have seen, interpret it. What do you think this passage means? Summarize the ideas. What do those add to your understanding? What does this passage say about God, about people and about faith?

Application

Knowing what the passage says, look for ways you can apply that to different areas of your life. How does this truth impact the way you live in your home, school, workplace, community, small group, church etc.?

Get Dusty

In confronting Satan's temptation, Jesus answered, "It is written: 'Man shall not live on bread alone, but on every word that comes from the mouth of God.'" (Matthew 4:4) A disciple finds strength gleaning spiritual food through the scriptures. You can find many different reading plans online. YouVersion is a Bible app where different reading plans are right there on your phone. I would encourage you to find a plan that takes you through the whole Bible in one year. Make a commitment every day to nourish your soul through his word.

Doer of God's Word

I was privileged to experience four years studying the Bible under some of the greatest teachers at Dallas Seminary. My biggest challenge though, was aligning my life to obey all the new things I was learning from scripture. Every day I learned something new but was still trying to apply what I had learned the day before. So much truth demanded so much change, and I must confess, at times I stopped obeying God's word. It felt like too much. Here I was at a school learning to preach to others, but I was lousy at preaching to myself.

The disciples learned how foolish it was to hear God's word but not put it into practice. Jesus shared the story of two very different men.

> Why do you call me, "Lord, Lord," and do not do what I say? As for everyone who comes to me and hears my words and puts them into practice, I will show you what they are like. They are like a man building a house, who dug down deep and laid the foundation on rock. When a flood came, the torrent struck that house but could not shake it, because it was well built. But the one who hears my words and does not put them into

*practice is like a man who built a house on the
ground without a foundation. The moment
the torrent struck that house, it collapsed and
its destruction was complete. (Luke 6:46-49)*

Obedience is not optional. It is what brings stability
and fruitful living to our lives. You can't have Jesus
simply as Savior. He must be Lord. When we put
Jesus' words into practice, life becomes unshakeable.
Notice Jesus did not say obedience will prevent us
from experiencing difficulty. He tells us storms will
come. Instead obedience will give us the tools and
the stability to keep our feet firmly planted even
in difficulty.

Hearing without obedience leads to deception. The
apostle James says, "Do not merely listen to the
word, and so deceive yourself. Do what it says."
(James 1:12) No one is surprised at what happens to
the foolish man except perhaps himself! Everyone
knows without a solid foundation the house will
collapse. So why do people build their lives on
deception, greed, pride, bitterness, doubt, anger,
worry and others? We know those are not
dependable when storms come. Yet we gravitate to
those all the time and this is because we are most
likely hearers not doers.

A disciple is always thinking of ways to apply

scripture to his life.

- Take one of those truths from this book already that you have not applied and make a commitment now to change.

- Pray that God would give you the strength to live that truth out every day. Here is where we can lean on the Holy Spirit, trusting as Jesus promised that the Spirit will remind us of the God's truths when they are needed. (John 14:26) When the Spirit brings a verse to mind, get excited because that is the Holy Spirit at work in you.

- Post the passages of scripture that speak to that issue in prominent places so you can be reminded. Better yet, memorize them. Psalm 119:11 says "I have hidden your word in my heart that I might not sin against you." How do you hide God's word in your heart? Memorize it!

- Find one person who will hold you accountable to making a change. It is best if that is the person who is discipling you or an individual in your small group. Give that person access to your life allowing them to ask difficult questions.

And be honest with them.

Get Dusty

Right now, today, is there a truth from God's word you know is not being applied in your life? Make the wise decision to do something about it. Find some people to help you and then watch how your faith stands strong through the darkest storm.

Communicator of God's Word

Jesus spoke with authority and people listened because his words were filled with truth given by God himself. "For I did not speak on my own, but the Father who sent me commanded me to say all that I have spoken." (John 12:49) Every word Jesus spoke came from the Father. If you want to talk like Jesus, the word of God has to be part of your conversation. I am not saying every word you say has to be from the Bible. Our conversations often range wider than that, but a disciple knows how to encourage and exhort one another with God's word at just the right time.

Jesus used scripture as a base to explain God's best for our lives. In the Sermon on the Mount, Jesus said,

> *You have heard that it was said to the people long ago, "You shall not murder, and anyone who murders will be subject to judgment." But I tell you that anyone who is angry with a brother or sister will be subject to judgment. (Matthew 5:21-22)*

He taught from God's word helping the listener understand fully what was meant. More than simply avoiding the outward act of murder, the truth God wanted us to understand was that hatred in our heart is just like murder. If the word of God doesn't touch the interior of your life, it will eventually show on the exterior.

He used scripture to determine best practices. Early in his ministry, Jesus was challenged.

> *While Jesus was having dinner at Matthew's house, many tax collectors and sinners came and ate with him and his disciples. When the Pharisees saw this, they asked his disciples, "Why does your teacher eat with tax collectors and sinners?" On hearing this, Jesus said, "It is not the healthy who need a doctor, but the sick. But go and learn what this means: 'I desire mercy, not sacrifice.' For I have not come to call the righteous, but sinners."*

His response came from the book of Hosea. While others were challenging his relationships, Jesus was speaking to the deep desire for mercy.

He used scripture to challenge people to live God's best for them. On two separate occasions, he went to the temple and saw the court of prayer being used as a marketplace. Jesus called the priests to live better by quoting Isaiah saying: "It is written," he said to them, "'My house will be called a house of prayer,' but you are making it 'a den of robbers.'" (Matthew 21:13) He invites the people there to see what God's original purpose was for that place in the temple and how they were missing the mark.

He used scripture to encourage people. He preached his first sermon in a small fishing town where he opens up Isaiah speaking about the life-giving ministry of the Messiah. After sitting down, He says "Today that scripture is being fulfilled in your hearing." Instead of angered, they were inspired. All spoke well of him and were amazed at the gracious words that came from his lips. (Luke 4:10a) The powerful proclamation of God's word brings strength and encouragement.

The disciples understood this and began to share God's word. When you read the sermons of Peter or hear the words of John, you know they are filled with Old Testament scripture. The challenge is knowing when to speak and what verses. In our culture today, people aren't prone to believing something just because it is in the Bible. The Bible doesn't mean that much to people anymore. But when we can share how those truths impact our lives, how they have guided us and how they have been a firm foundation, the Bible will have power for us and others.

Get Dusty

Share with someone else one thing from God's word that has excited you lately. Why did it encourage or challenge you? What impact has it had? How has it changed your life? Pray that your excitement will become their excitement and be encouraged by the way the power of God's word changes others.

Possessor of a Biblical Worldview

"People function on the basis of their worldview more consistently than even they themselves may realize. The problem is not outward things. The problem is having, and then acting upon, the right worldview – the worldview which gives men and women the truth of what is." Francis Schaeffer

A worldview is the sum of what we believe about the purpose of life, the nature of people, the scope of spirituality and the destiny of humanity. This becomes the lens through which we make our decisions, steward our resources, prioritize our life and choose our friendships. Every day, our worldview is being influenced by the media, close friends and family, our experiences and what we read. What we believe about our world is a major factor in how we choose to live, and how we develop our worldview is critical. Where we get truth from matters. As Schaeffer says, we all have a worldview of some type and followers of Jesus choose to follow him, in part, because we want to adopt his worldview.

Jesus taught the disciples that the scriptures are the source of truth. Our best opportunity to have a Christian worldview is to have a worldview that is based upon the scriptures. A disciple chooses to approach the world not through the lens of culture or what is popular, but looks at the world through the lens of God's word. Jesus powerfully stood on God's word and taught the disciples to use the scriptures as an ongoing authority for their life.

Jesus used the scriptures as basis for his life. Never once did he contract an Old Testament passage. He did not say they were obsolete or not worth reading. In quoting them, he affirmed that every word was from God. He had memorized the word and knew it right down to the verb tenses and each word. (John 7:15) He treated the Old Testament as historical fact, and its heroes were historical figures to Jesus. (Matthew 7:37-39) He knew the power of the scriptures, using them to combat Satan's temptations. (Luke 16: 29) He knew people would believe it more than signs. To this day, one word of scripture can affect more change in a person's life than a myriad of miracles. (Luke 16:31) He urged people to read it, know it, value it and live it. (Mark 12:26)

More than just quoting the Bible though, he subjected himself to it. Jesus obeyed the word of God first. He knew the Bible was God's word and that true life came from following every word that the Father had written. He followed the Ten

Commandments honoring the Sabbath and participating in worship to make it holy. He submitted to the governing authorities over him. He loved his neighbor as himself. He forgave his enemies on the cross. He used the scriptures to interpret his world instead of trying to use the world to interpret the Bible. It is through God's word that we understand who the Father is, who Jesus is, and what salvation has done for us. We don't let other broken and deceived people tell us what sin is, we let God's word do that.

A disciple chooses not to see the world as others see it because it is popular or easy, but commits themselves to seeing the world as God created it. This creates conflict.

- Our world says we earn it, so money is ours. A Biblical worldview says it belongs to him.
- Our world says to make choices based on what will bring you the most happiness, a Biblical worldview says we choose what honors God most.
- Our world says life matters only if it is wanted, a Biblical worldview says life matters because we are all formed in the image of God.
- Our world says it doesn't matter what you believe, as long as you believe it strongly, a

Biblical worldview says there is truth
to believe.

Our worldview determines our priorities, our
choices, our spending and our values.
To discern a biblical worldview is a lifelong endeavor
and leads to countercultural living. In the end, I find
people are often attracted to counter-cultural living
and that in itself provides an openness to sharing
Christ with others.

Get Dusty

Ask God to make you aware of when society's
worldview is at odds with the Bible's. Ask yourself
where your worldview may differ. As you read the
scriptures, be open to letting the word change your
set of life assumptions.

Conclusion

When you begin to think, "I cannot do that," you are in a great place. Let me be clear. You can't. You yourself cannot do any of it. The mystery of the gospel is that Christ comes alive in us. And Christ in us can do more than we can imagine. Get to know the Christ who is in you. Rest on the Christ who is in you. Align the sails of your life so the Christ in you can be your hope. Put on the armor of the cross so Christ in you can stand firm when the enemy attacks. Abide in the Savior. Listen in prayer.

CHAPTER 4

HANDS - Reaching Out Like Jesus

When the disciples answered Jesus' call to follow him, I wonder if they had any idea the unusual and uncomfortable places he would take them for the sake of the gospel. Did they expect Jesus would take them to the homes of prostitutes and tax collectors? Did they expect to leave the safety of their confined Jewish area to roam where Gentiles lived? Were they prepared to come face-to-face in confrontation with the Jerusalem elite?

Jesus' hands touched a lot of people. He touched and healed a leper. His hands wrote something in the sand that caused men to leave the woman caught in adultery alone. His hands held goblets in the homes of undesirables. The disciples learned their hands must reach out to others as the hands of Jesus did.

If you ever wonder how Christianity spread so fast, this is the answer. Those twelve knew that a disciple does not follow simply for their spiritual and eternal well-being. A disciple knows they have this high calling to advance the kingdom of light into the darkness.

A disciple reaches as Jesus reached.

Developing a Heart for the Lost

The spiritually lost were always at the forefront of Jesus' mind. They had seen Jesus teach and demonstrate that God's priority for the lost should be a disciples' priority. In fact, during a meeting with the greedy and disliked tax collector, Zacchaeus, Jesus reminded people of his personal mission statement. "For the Son of Man came to seek and to save the lost." (Luke 19:10)

In Luke 15, Jesus told stories about a lost sheep, a lost coin and a lost son. Each story spoke of the profound sense of loss the people experienced, their desperate attempt to find that which was lost and not only their rejoicing, but the rejoicing in heaven when a lost person is found.

Jesus follows that up in Luke 16 by teaching us to use our resources to reach the lost. Understanding the true value of lost people finding their spiritual home, a disciple will do what they can with their resources to win them over to the gospel. (Luke 16:9)

Jesus modeled going to places where he could reach the lost. He went to Samaria to reach a lost woman. He went to the Gadarenes to reach a man lost among the demonically-possessed. He went to

138

Jericho to look up Zacchaeus who was lost in his greed. He reached out to the Pharisees and Sadducees who were lost in their religiosity. He went to the homes of those who were considered the most lost, like the tax collectors, prostitutes and sinners, to bring them joy and hope. The disciples had signed up to follow a rabbi who would teach them how to pray, how to draw near to God and how to have a fruitful life. Next this rabbi would take them to parties with the outcasts. They learned the lost are a priority.

After years of persecuting Christians, Paul grew a heart for the lost that humbles me. He writes to the church in Rome:

> I have great sorrow and unceasing anguish in my heart. For I could wish that I myself were cursed and cut off from Christ for the sake of my people, those of my own race, the people of Israel. Theirs is the adoption to sonship; theirs the divine glory, the covenants, the receiving of the law, the temple worship and the promises.
> (Romans 9:2-4)

Paul's heart so breaks for the lostness of Israel, he wishes he could trade his own salvation for theirs. He was even willing to be cursed so they could be saved.

Most people I know have a heart cold toward the

lost but warm toward anything that leads to a comfortable life. They have hearts for more success or for more happiness. Right now, you may have to take that cross you are carrying and put that old heart to death in order to grow a heart for the lost. How do you do grow that heart for the lost?

- First, make sure you are being discipled by someone who has a heart that is broken for the lost. Their heart will ignite yours.

- Second, pray that God would change your heart. You can't do it by trying harder. God has to break it.

- Third, remember what you have been saved and spared from because of Jesus. Where would your life be without Christ? What has Jesus done for you? Without a sense of your own lostness and salvation, you will never have a heart for the lost.

- Fourth, personalize the lost. Jesus knew where each person's lostness would take them. They would be eternally separated from him. They would never have the life or eternity God had planned for them. We tend to think that professional, middle class suburbanites are not lost. They are missing out. Begin to see family members, friends and coworkers as Jesus sees them. Lost. Pray that breaks your heart.

Having a heart for the lost demands that we do something. Jesus trained his disciples specifically to go and reach the lost.

Get Dusty

Jesus looked over Jerusalem one day and wept at the lostness of the people. Ask God to break your heart for the lost right now. Write down the names of five people who are far from Christ. Pray regularly that the Holy Spirit would move in their life and that they would seek a relationship with Christ.

Sharing Christ with the Lost

He intentionally sent the disciples and about 60 others into towns to prepare the way for people to receive Jesus. They were to knock on doors, perform miracles and proclaim the reality of the kingdom of God. He gave them these instructions.

When you enter a town and are welcomed, eat what is offered to you. Heal the sick who are there and tell them, "The kingdom of God has come near to you." (Luke 10:8-9)

I am convinced most people don't share the gospel, not because they are afraid of what people will say, but because they don't believe they can do it right. They would rather not share than mess it up.

Notice that Jesus trained and equipped the disciples to share the good news. Ask someone to train you on sharing the gospel. Watch how they share. Hear their experiences. Even practice on them. There are a number of easy-to-remember presentations of the gospel. One that I find helpful is one I shared in the first chapter about the gospel. This one focuses on good news which people want to hear about.

The bad news is that we have all sinned and

fallen short of God's desire for us. (Romans 3:23) The bad news gets worse because the wages of that sin are death and we are separated from God. (Romans 6:23)

But there is good news. While we were yet sinners, Christ died for us. He received the wages for sin that we should have received. (Romans 5:8) And the good news gets even better. We can receive what Christ has done through faith. We trust in him alone for forgiveness and salvation. This is not a religion where we have to earn our salvation, it is all grace. (Ephesians 2:8-9)

The disciples saw firsthand the power of one's testimony. People can certainly argue with the gospel, but it is difficult to argue with someone's testimony. What helped launch the kingdom was the interest people had in the gospel because someone had shared their testimony.

The woman at the well went back to the village to share about Jesus and the whole village came to see Jesus. (John 4)

The demoniac freed of many spirits ran back to the town sharing what Jesus did. The people came out to see Jesus because they could not believe the testimony. (Mark 5)

Jesus healed a man born blind. People saw that he no longer needed to beg and wondered what had happened to him. His healing created such controversy because he was healed on the Sabbath. Many in the city came to hear how this man had been healed by Jesus. His testimony was simple: "Once I was blind," he said, "and now I can see." And what made the difference was Jesus. (John 9)

Never underestimate the power of your testimony. Take some time to prepare it and write it down. It is helpful to have both a one-minute version you can share at any moment and a longer one that shares more fully all Jesus has done.

If you have never written one, a simple way to start is to talk about three things.

- Describe what your life was like before you met Jesus.

- Talk about the defining moment when you met Jesus. How did you hear and what caused you to invite him into your heart?

- Describe the difference Jesus has made in your life.

Get Dusty

Now that you have an idea of how to share the gospel and your testimony, pray for opportunities to share it. Ask the Father every day to bring someone into your path who needs to know your story and pray for those opportunities.

What keeps people from sharing the gospel is the fear that people will ask questions they are ill-equipped for. There are common objections to the gospel. The disciples understood this. They were questioned all the time about why Jesus did something. They learned to be prepared to give an answer. In fact, Peter instructs us to do the same.

> *But in your hearts revere Christ as Lord. Always be prepared to give an answer to everyone who asks you to give the reason for the hope that you have. But do this with gentleness and respect. (1 Peter 3:15)*

To be able to reach people as Jesus reached, we have to be able to defend significant areas of faith. We, by ourselves, cannot change a person's thinking, but we can tell people that we have not left our brains at the door to follow Jesus.

Defending the Existence of God

I have met many people who just believe in something, but they don't know how to defend it. They just know there is a God, but have no way of helping someone else find that same sense of conviction. There is not enough space here to write a full argument for God's existence, but there are four revelations of God that lead us to believe he exists.

I. God reveals himself in the cosmos

Centuries ago, if you asked people whether God exists, they would point to the heavens. David wrote in Psalm 19: 1-2: "The heavens declare the glory of God; the skies proclaim the work of his hands. Day after day they pour forth speech; night after night they reveal knowledge."

How did the universe get here? Either it has always existed or it was started. Most respected scientists and astronomers believe the universe had an actual beginning. If it had a beginning, then something or someone must have created it, since logically something does not come from nothingness.

So, if the universe has not always existed and if nothing cannot create something, then that leaves a third option that someone or something created the universe. An eternal power beyond the universe caused it to come into existence. This doesn't prove that God himself exists but that a greater power had to create the universe.

II. God reveals himself in the intricacies of planet earth

A second indicator that a creator exists is the incredible way earth has all the right conditions for life. Some describe it as the very "fine tuning" of the universe.

Dr. Francis Collins, former head of the Human Genome Project, says that if any of the constants of oxygen, light, water, or warmth was off by even one in a millionth, there would be no galaxy, stars, planets or people. David Page, a Princeton Science Professor said that the odds of the universe randomly taking a form that is suitable to life is on in 10,000,000,000 to the 124th power. (One in ten billion to the 24th power). That is such a huge number, leading people to believe a creative force must have existed. (Ravi Zacharias, The End of Reason, p. 35)

Not only are the exact conditions for life in the universe overwhelming, but Francis Crick, one of the two scientists who discovered DNA, was overwhelmed by biological life's own complexity. He describes DNA as a massive computer program and storage system. He estimated the odds that intelligent life existed on earth as the result of chance...would be 1 in 10 to the 2 billionth. (Gary Habermas, The Case for the Resurrection, p 179) While it is possible that life just happened, the odds that it came by chance are astronomical; and the possibility that life evolved continually through stages without dying out are equally astounding.

III. God is revealed through moral conscience

Without God, there would be no need for morality. To use the words that Sartre attributed to Dostoyevsky, "If there is no God, then everything is permissible." If God does not exist, then I don't need to worry about morality. Why should I care about people if we are accidents that just happened? The fact that there are moral laws and that not everything is permissible, proves that God exists. But he has also revealed himself through our conscience, that little interior device that helps us determine right from wrong.

IV. God has revealed himself through Christ

Some have suggested if God wanted us to believe in

him, then why wouldn't he just appear to us? Think about it though, a creator God appearing to us. How would that be? John MacArthur once said that if God were to appear: we would expect him to be sinless; we would expect him to be holy; we would expect his words to be the greatest words ever spoken; we would expect him to exert a profound power over human personality; we would expect him to perform supernatural doings; and we would expect him to manifest the love of God. That was Jesus. He meets all that criteria.

Is it reasonable to believe God exists? Definitely. We are not accidents but people made in his image for his purposes.

Get Dusty

Review these points again and again to become familiar with them. You may want to write a few points down to have on your phone or in your wallet to look at when you are engaged in a conversation. Practice sharing these with someone else and be encouraged when people listen.

Defending the Authority of Scripture to Reach Others

The uniqueness of the Bible is undeniable. It was written over a period of 1,600 years by 40 authors on three continents and yet speaks of a singular story. Its unity is unparalleled as evidenced by *The Whole Story* series from Calvary Church. The sheer fact that so many different authors wrote a continuation of the same story speaks of its uniqueness.

That unity is a result of each of those authors being inspired through the Holy Spirit. Paul says that the scriptures were God-breathed and useful for teaching, rebuking, correcting and training in righteousness. (II Timothy 3:16) The Holy Spirit superintended the writing of each of the 66 books by various human authors, allowing them to write according to their personalities, while ensuring each word in the original manuscript was the exact word God wanted. The Holy Spirit continues to be active in using biblical truth to shape us.

The Bible is also unparalleled in its preservation. Since we do not have the original scrolls that Moses or Matthew penned, it makes people wonder if the scrolls we do have are what the original authors intended to write or if they have been amended to reflect people's beliefs. The first copies of some of the New Testament books date from about 50 years after the originals were completed. The gap between the original writing of the history of Rome by Tacitus and the first copies is 1000 years. We do have over 14,000 full or partial early manuscripts of the Bible. That is a lot to compare and contrast. There is incredible accuracy among them. Given that they were copies of copies, there are relatively few mistakes. No other works compare to those. In fact, Homer's Iliad has the next most copies coming in at only 643. God made sure that we had lots of copies of his word to assure us it is trustworthy. Compared to other ancient manuscripts, there is more than enough evidence to assure us we accurately have what God intended.

The Bible is unparalleled in the ability to check its facts with history. A common accusation is that following the years Jesus lived, myths and legends about his abilities arose. The gospel writers then recorded a mix of both facts and legend in their writing leaving us uncertain today about what Jesus really did. Given the timing and the opposition to Jesus that is unlikely. The gospel of Mark was written in 70 AD, only 40 years after the events happened. At the time of its writing, there were still people alive who were eyewitnesses to the life and ministry of

Jesus, including hostile eyewitnesses who could have served as a corrective if false teachers were going around. Don't you think that people who were still alive would have said these things were fabrications? Alexander the Great died in 323 BC, yet the first biography of his life wasn't written until 400 years later. The first written records of Buddha were 350 years after his death. The first records of Mohammed, the founder of Islam, were composed 125 years after his death. God made sure what we know about Jesus was written at a time when people could have verified the text.

Finally, the Bible is unparalleled in its affirmation from other historical sources. The Jewish Talmud and the Koran of Islam both support details of Jesus' life written in scripture. Of all the books that could possibly try to discredit Jesus, these would be the top two, and instead they offer support. There are hundreds of historical events recorded in scripture. Archaeologists have tried to discredit the Bible by proving some of its history wrong. While not every historical event has been validated by history, not one bit of evidence has occurred to undermine what the Bible has said.

If we are to reach our world for Christ, we have to be able to speak wisely and with authority and knowledge. For me, and I am sure for you, no book speaks to the heart of humanity like the Bible. No book helps people make wise choices like the scriptures. Offering great comfort and wisdom, the Bible is unparalleled in its ability to change lives and transform communities.

Get Dusty

You may want to pick up a book on apologetics. So much more information is available on how to defend our faith. Thank God for the way the Bible has been preserved and for its power in changing lives.

Defending the Uniqueness of Jesus

Lots of people are intrigued by Jesus and even like the teachings of Jesus, but struggle with his exclusivity. They argue that Jesus may be a way to God and may even be the best way to know God, but say it would be unfair of God to only have one way to him. A disciple gives their life to follow their master because they believe they have the words of eternal life. That Jesus is the only way to God is exclusive, but Christianity is very inclusive because anyone, regardless of their background, can find rest in him.

In today's postmodern world, a disciple needs to be prepared to share why they follow Jesus as the way to God.

The exclusivity of Jesus is not based on what Christians choose to believe, but is based on what Jesus said about himself.

I. Jesus claimed to be God

Jesus claimed to continue the work of God.

> *So, because Jesus was doing these things on the Sabbath, the Jewish leaders began to persecute him. In his defense Jesus said to them, "My Father is always at his work to this*

very day, and I too am working." For this reason they tried all the more to kill him; not only was he breaking the Sabbath, but he was even calling God his own Father, making himself equal with God." (John 5:16-18)

Jesus claimed to forgive sin as God. When a lame man was lowered in front of him from the roof of a house, Jesus forgave the man and then healed him as proof that he could forgive. The people present knew that this was an assertion that he was God. (Mark 2:6-7)

Jesus claimed to have a heavenly origin. Jesus told a crowd that he had stood in the presence of the Father. He claimed to share in the glory of his Father. He talked about being in the presence of the Father when the earth began. Jesus said that his home was in heaven. "No one has ever gone into heaven except the one who came from heaven—the Son of Man." (John 3:13)

Jesus claimed to God's name. He claimed to be the God of the Old Testament while ascribing the sacred name, "I Am" to himself. When Moses stood before the burning bush and asked God who was speaking to him, God replied that his name was.... I AM. Jesus referred to himself many times as "I AM." He said, I am the bread of life; I am the light of the world; I am the resurrection and the life. I am the great shepherd. His audiences clearly understood that he was claiming to be God by taking this name.

Jesus claimed to have authority over eternal life. Jesus told Martha after Lazarus died: "I am the resurrection and the life. The one who believes in me will live, even though they die." (John 11:25) Jesus claimed authority over this life and over eternal life.

II. Possible conclusions about those claims

C.S. Lewis wrote that, knowing Jesus made these claims to be God, there can only be one of three conclusions about Jesus:

He is a liar. If he is not God and did not continue the work of God, then the claims are false and he is a liar, and the most evil of liars for trying to intentionally deceive people.

He is a lunatic. If Jesus was not intentionally deceiving people, then either he was self-deluded or deceived. Today, he would be labeled as mentally ill. It is difficult to imagine millions of people following someone who was so mentally disturbed.

He is Lord. If Jesus is of sound mind and was telling the truth, then he must be Lord. He must be who he claimed to be.

The resurrection however, proves he is Lord.

III. The resurrection proves his claims

Jesus claimed his body would be destroyed and that he would rise again three days later. Not only did he claim it, but he rose from the dead. Everything hangs on the resurrection. His body was sealed into a known grave and then was no longer there. Had the Romans hidden the body, they would have reproduced it later. Had the disciples stolen the body, it is highly doubtful they would have undergone such harsh persecution knowing it was all a hoax. In fact, the changed lives of the disciples that caused them to risk their lives is what gives the most credence to the fact Jesus rose from the dead.

If he fulfilled that claim, then he can be trusted to fulfill all his other claims. It was Jesus himself who argued he was the way: "Jesus answered, "I am the way and the truth and the life. No one comes to the Father except through me." (John 14:6)

Get Dusty

Keep reviewing these points until you are

comfortable with them. Talk about them with someone. Write them down where they are easily accessible. The next time the conversation comes up, pray for boldness to ask a few questions and share a few things.

Willing to Discuss the Dilemma
of God and Suffering

Jesus was not afraid to dialogue with the disciples about the pain and suffering of life. They wrestled with the brutal death of John the Baptist. They talked about what the source of a man's blindness might be. (John 9) A disciple who wants to reach as Jesus reaches can't shy away from talking about the painful situations of life, but needs to be able to engage in the conversation.

I. We have a Suffering God

We do have a suffering God. Jesus' own suffering is important to this conversation. Jesus was not just a man or an angel, he was also fully God. From a Christian perspective, the God we accuse when we have been hurt, the God who bears the brunt of all our questions is a God who himself chose to become the greatest victim of evil ever. The God who created this universe is the God who suffers with us.

II. We have to trust there is purpose in pain

Then the question becomes why would a God who knows the pain and hurt of suffering allow it to continue? To answer that question, we should look at two differing arguments for suffering.

The Philosophical Argument

Wrestling with the problem of evil, the philosopher David Hume said if God is willing to prevent evil, but does not prevent it then he cannot be an almighty god. He must be impotent. If he is able to prevent suffering, but chooses not to do it, then he must be malevolent. If He is both able and willing but does nothing with evil, then he must himself be evil.

This argument looks at the two important attributes of God, his power and his goodness. Perhaps a way to frame this is in the following equation:

- If God is great, then he must have the power to remove evil.
- If God is good, then he must want to remove evil.
- Therefore, evil must not exist.

But since evil does exist, what does that mean? Either God does not exist or he is not really God at all.

The Bible offers a different argument.

One of the phrases often used in this discussion is a phrase about the best possible world. We want to live in a best possible world. We think that God originally created the best possible world, but it doesn't feel like the best possible world. When we think of that best possible world, we really think about a world that exists for us and our happiness. We think of a world that is pain-free without troubles or difficulties.

Jesus promised the disciples that the best possible world is coming. Heaven is the perfect world that God has prepared for us. At that time, there will be no more mourning or pain or suffering. If God's desire is that we would know him and have a relationship with him and understand that we can fully trust him, then is it possible that this world could be designed for that? Either God created this world unaware of how powerful evil is and he is not powerful over it, or God was powerful enough to create a world where the allowance of evil and the result of suffering might have value.

A new equation might be:

- If God is great, he must have the power to bring about the best possible world.
- If God is good, he must want to bring about the best possible world in the best way.

- Allowing evil, temporarily, must be the best way to bring about the best world.

Jesus promised the disciples he was going to prepare a place for them in that better world. (John 14) The hope of a better world is heaven. Had God not already done that in creating Eden? What is the difference between Eden and Heaven? Eden was paradise but it had a tempting serpent. In a perfect world, there will be no serpent. Eden was a perfect world, but it was not the best of all worlds because evil had not yet been vanquished. The best of all worlds is a place where now knowing the difference between good and evil, we choose the good, and we choose God knowing that evil is forever defeated.

To one who is suffering in the moment that may not be consolation, but it takes us back to the reminder we have a suffering God. Jesus who experienced great persecution and pain eagerly desires to enter into our suffering. A disciple chooses to walk with people through their suffering as a tangible expression of the presence of Christ.

Get Dusty

People are more inclined to hear what we have to

say when they know how much we really care. Before trying to explain suffering, care for the sufferer. Enter into their life. Offer practical assistance. Let them see the love of a suffering God through you.

Using my Spiritual Gifts to Reach Others

At the end of their discipleship journey, Jesus made a startling prediction to his followers. "Very truly I tell you, whoever believes in me will do the works I have been doing, and they will do even greater things than these, because I am going to the Father." (John 14:12) Having seen Jesus heal the sick, teach great crowds, still the storms, feed thousands and free the spiritually-oppressed, Jesus was now telling them they would do greater things! What would that mean? Jesus was going to send the Holy Spirit who would gift them with divine empowerments to serve. A spiritual gift is a God-given ability to serve. It is used not to build the person up, but to build up the kingdom of God. What is a disciple to understand about spiritual gifts?

<u>A disciple knows about spiritual gifts</u>

To the church in Corinth, Paul challenged believers to know their gifts. "Now about the gifts of the Spirit, brothers and sisters, I do not want you to be uninformed." (I Corinthians 12:1)

Throughout scripture there are about 20 different gifts that are listed.

There are ministry gifts distributed throughout
164

believers which include the gifts of wisdom, knowledge, discernment, faith, prophecy, teaching, helps, hospitality, administration, encouragement, giving, leadership, and intercession along with specific leadership gifts of pastor, evangelist, and apostle.

There are miraculous gifts that are given from time to time to allow God to work including gifts of miracles, healing, speaking in tongues and interpretation of tongues.

A disciple knows they have a spiritual gift

A disciple knows God has gifted them with one or two particular spiritual gifts. The moment the Holy Spirit comes into our lives, he gives us the ability to serve. Sometimes the Holy Spirit takes our natural gifts and abilities and energizes them to serve in the kingdom. Other times the Holy Spirit brings forth new gifts to help us build the kingdom.

I often hear people say they can recognize spiritual gifts in the life of another person, but they did not get a gift. Paul writes that every person receives a spiritual gift as the result of the Spirit's indwelling. "Now to each one the manifestation of the Spirit is given for the common good." (I Corinthians 12:7) If you don't know your gift, then there are a number of online assessments to review. They will lead you to understanding how God has equipped you for service.

A disciple actively uses their gift

Paul says a spiritual gift is given not to glorify ourselves or advance our standing, but for the common good of building Christ's kingdom. The church needs your gift. A disciple actively looks for ways to use their gift. They find people around them who can help them use the gift in the most effective way. Are you using your talents to build up your portfolio or using your spiritual gifts to build the kingdom? You may need to take out that cross and put to death some of your own self-advancement.

One caution. No particular spiritual gift is better than another. In fact, all the gifts are needed to accomplish the building of the kingdom. Because we often see the world through our spiritual gift, we tend to think our gift is better than others. Teachers think there should be more teaching. Evangelists think there should be more evangelism. Those with the gift of helps accuse others of not helping. All the gifts are needed and when they work together, the body of Christ is healthy and the church reflects Jesus.

When the church is healthy and reflecting Jesus, it affects the world around it and the gates of hell cannot come against it.

Get Dusty

Take a spiritual gifts inventory to determine what your gifts might be. Find ways within the church and your small group to use those gifts. The Spirit gave them to you to use!

Using My Resources to Reach Others

Martin Luther argued that a disciple had three conversions. There had to first be a conversion of one's heart and then a conversion of one's mind. The third was a conversion of their pocketbook. If Christ does not have access to our money and resources, he is not our Lord. Committed to building this kingdom and discipling others, a disciple willingly uses their resources to support that work.

Proverbs says that we are to honor the Lord with the first fruits of what we have. "Honor the Lord with your wealth, with the first fruits of all your crops; then your barns will be filled to overflowing, and your vats will brim over with new wine." (Proverbs 3:9–10) When we do that, he will cause there to be an overflow in our life.

I hear a lot of people who want to honor God in their life, their marriage, their workplace, their school or their singleness. I am amazed how people want to honor God in many areas of their life, but not with their treasure. Unfortunately, this shows the true nature of their hearts, for Jesus said that where our treasure is, our hearts will be also. (Matthew 6:21)

The Old Testament is specific about giving a tenth to

God. In fact, when you look at all the Jewish people tithed on, it ended up being greater than ten percent. The New Testament is silent on the amount or the percentage. Everything does belong to God, but if a tenth was the benchmark in the Old Testament, it should be the minimum for us in this season of grace since generosity does some things.

Giving generously breaks the financial bondage of the enemy. I have seldom seen a person generous with their money who is in bondage to money.

Giving advances the kingdom of God. Learning the importance of generosity from Jesus, the disciples called the early church to radical generosity. Barnabas sold some property and gave it to the disciples in an incredible act of obedience. Without the generosity of people, the early church would not have been able to feed the poor, support its leaders who then help its members in need. The radical generosity of Christians allowed the church to prosper.

Giving produces a harvest. Giving to God should not be seen as a loss, rather as a planting. A farmer plants seeds in the ground that will eventually die, but there will be great fruit from that. The same is true with our generosity. The Bible says that the one who sows generously reaps generously.

"Remember this: Whoever sows sparingly will also reap sparingly, and whoever sows generously will also reap generously. Each of you should give what you have decided in your heart to give, not reluctantly or under compulsion, for God loves a cheerful giver. And God is able to bless you abundantly, so that in all things at all times, having all that you need, you will abound in every good work. As it is written: "They have freely scattered their gifts to the poor;
  their righteousness endures forever." Now he who supplies seed to the sower and bread for food will also supply and increase your store of seed and will enlarge the harvest of your righteousness. (2 Corinthians 9:6-10)

What is the harvest? The harvest one reaps begins with righteousness. When we are generous, God keeps the destroyer away. Money slips through our fingers at times. We can have a healthy sum in the bank account but a few repairs, an unexpected trip and some medical bills can eat away at the nest egg. God promises in Malachi 3 that our giving spiritually protects us from the enemy stealing our precious resources. I have seen that with my own finances. I am not afraid to say that when I do the math on my personal expenses, it does not add up. I should have way less. Tithing may not mean that you will get rich, but it does mean that God protects what is left.

The harvest is also more seed to be generous with. You will hear people teaching that if you give more money, God will give you more for you to enjoy. Were that true, then there would be no poverty in the developing world. You cannot deny Paul says there is a blessing that is proportional to the planting, but he is careful to tell us that we won't reap more harvest for our own selfish pleasure. We are disciples with an allegiance to a new kingdom. God gives increase so that it is used as seed sown in greater generosity.

Get Dusty

I invite you again to lay out your finances before the Lord. Are you using them for kingdom purposes? Are you growing in generosity? You may not be able to give ten percent right now, but is your generosity building your faith? Are you being stretched more and more in your trust through your giving? Are you eager to see your resources used in some way to advance the kingdom?

A disciple reaches with their life and their pocketbook. You may need bring the cross of Christ between you and the fear of trusting God with your resources.

Making Disciples Who Will Reach the World

Then the eleven disciples went to Galilee, to the mountain where Jesus had told them to go. When they saw him, they worshiped him; but some doubted. Then Jesus came to them and said, "All authority in heaven and on earth has been given to me. Therefore go and make disciples of all nations, baptizing them in the name of the Father and of the Son and of the Holy Spirit, and teaching them to obey everything I have commanded you. And surely, I am with you always, to the very end of the age." (Matthew 28:16-20)

It is known as the Great Commission. These last words of Jesus to the disciples commissioned them to make disciples. All along they were ministering and sharing. But Jesus gave them an intentional initiative to disciple others. They were not recipients of God's grace, they were to be carriers of it. They were not followers only of Jesus, they were to disciple others. They were called for a greater purpose. Now they were to fulfill that purpose.

Every time I reach someone with the good news of Jesus, I have a new responsibility to make sure they are discipled. We are called to share our faith and ultimately to disciple people. The cost of not discipling is high. I think of Chris, who years ago I lead to Christ in my parent's living room. I went off to university. He went to another school, and no one ever discipled him. Now he is a social media advocate for atheism. That is why a few months ago when Joe gave his life to Christ in my office, I knew that I had to follow up. Now we may not physically be able to disciple every person ourselves, but we do have a responsibility to make sure someone is helping them become like Christ.

I am sure the disciples felt ill-equipped for that task. That was exactly where God wanted them to be. But Jesus had given them everything they needed. They had the head, heart, hands and feet of the savior. And they had the Holy Spirit.

You are more equipped for the task of making disciples than you know. You have the Holy Spirit guiding and leading you to multiply your faith and what you have learned into someone else.

I trust as you reflect upon your life now at the end of this journey, you are amazed at how dusty you have become. Christ has formed you from the inside out. Your head is more like his, as are your heart, your hands and your feet. Now duplicate that experience with another. You have the resources. Simply walk through this book with them. Everything in here is foundational for helping them become a follower of Jesus.

Disciple-making was not optional in Jesus' command. It was not to be done when convenient. It is what disciples do. They make more disciples!

Get Dusty

Pick up your cross and put to death the fear of not being good enough, and invite someone to follow Jesus through you. May the same power that raised Jesus from the dead, be with you.

Conclusion

Following the resurrection of Jesus, the disciples gave themselves fully to the task of reaching others for Christ and making disciples. They sacrificed their resources; used their spiritual gifts; proclaimed the truths of the gospel and engaged in difficult conversations. They were able to reach those in high positions and the humble. They reached beyond economic and ethnic boundaries. They reached as far across the globe as they could.

Now we pick up that same mission.

Who is God calling you to reach? I challenge you to ask yourself that question each day. It might mean walking across a room or a street to reach someone. It could be picking up a phone or sending a text. It may be sacrificing your resources. Who is that person? Now, ask Jesus what they need? Do they need a clear explanation of the gospel, or do they simply need to see the gospel in action in your life? Would a book on apologetics be a vehicle for God's Holy Spirit to work in their lives? Now pray for them. We can prepare the way for Jesus to work, but we can't change a person. Only he can. Pray that the Spirit of Jesus would touch that person.

67173703R00099

Made in the USA
Lexington, KY
03 September 2017